People Skills for Library Managers

PEOPLE SKILLS FOR LIBRARY MANAGERS

A Common Sense Guide for Beginners

Lucile Wilson

1996
LIBRARIES UNLIMITED, INC.
Englewood, Colorado

*This book is dedicated to my husband Henry
and my daughters, Cheri and Martha.*

LIBRARIES UNLIMITED, INC.
P.O. Box 6633
Englewood, CO 80155-6633
1-800-237-6124

Library of Congress Cataloging-in-Publication Data

Wilson, Lucile.
    People skills for library managers : a common sense guide
for beginners / Lucile Wilson.
    xii, 125 p. 17x25 cm.
    Includes bibliographical references
    ISBN 1-56308-143-1
    1. Library personnel management--United States.
2. Interpersonal relations--United States. 3. Library
administration--United States.
    I. Title.
Z682.2.U5W55 1996
023'.9--dc20   94-39546
                                                    CIP

P

In order to keep this title in print and available to the academic community, this edition
was produced using digital reprint technology in a relatively short print run. This would
not have been attainable using traditional methods. Although the cover has been changed
from its original appearance, the text remains the same and all materials and methods
used still conform to the highest book-making standards.

Contents

Preface

For several years, I listened to people in the library profession, particularly supervisors in public libraries and school library media centers, express the need for a handbook on people skills. These supervisors expressed special interest in learning skills for managing their programs and staffs successfully and enhancing their leadership capabilities.

Most library managers today realize that they need to be more effective leaders. The survival of their programs and positions depends on their knowledge and use of people skills. They do not want theory but rather a practical guide with real-life examples and applications. Library schools, if they teach people skills at all, don't emphasize them for library managers. Although there are many books on management, leadership, organizational behavior, and communication skills, there is a need for a publication that addresses the specific people skills required by a school library media specialist, public librarian, university librarian, or librarian in a special library.

I've prepared this handbook to give library managers a practical, easy-to-read reference. I gleaned information from my 25 years as a school library media specialist and from various university courses, professional workshops, business meetings, management seminars, and books. This handbook offers straight talk for effective leadership on topics such as time management, planning, communications, power, motivation, and conflict resolution. It takes an interpersonal skills approach and provides practical examples of fundamental techniques. It presents an overview of the management process and shows how to apply specific skills to the library management profession.

I believe that applying the information in this handbook will enhance the professional and personal lives of library managers. Good luck and best wishes for better communications and more effective leadership!

Introduction

Because library managers spend so much time working with people, it seems reasonable for library school programs to devote significant training to the development of people skills. However, few library managers take courses in undergraduate or graduate school on how to work with people, and only a few attend workshops on this subject. Robert Wedgeworth, in *Libraries in the '90s*, states

> But the leadership in our field revolves around the ability to lead in collaborative arrangements, to persuade people to follow a particular course of action, and to get the work done through others. . . . If you're not effective in handling people, you won't be effective in handling the operation. We have not done the best job in our schools in training librarians to handle personnel. This is one of the areas that we have to strengthen in our curriculum for the next decade. (Riggs and Sabine 1988)

Library managers provide the necessary link between a library program and the users served by the program, and effective people skills are critical to a successful program. Library managers need people skills to meet the "information power" requirements of teachers, supervisors, principals, administrators, parents, students, and the community.

Because electronic access to information is not locally available in many communities, a motivated and enthusiastic library staff is important in providing information to the library patron. Good people skills compensate for lack of resources, but no amount of resources compensate for poor people skills.

Every library manager, moreover, markets programs, services, ideas, and resources, and they interact constantly with people. Library managers need interpersonal skills to create belief in the service they promote.

The largest allocation of funds in a library budget is for personnel. To handle the operations of a library effectively, a library manager must handle people effectively. Library managers need to select talented people who are willing to carry out the day-to-day operations. They must motivate, persuade, manage conflicts, delegate, solve problems, build teams, and establish a rapport with each individual. They also train staff and provide ongoing education to make the best use of resources.

All is for naught if a leader cannot promote the potential of the library. It makes no difference if a library has the greatest collection of materials, the most efficient and newest technology, an attractive facility, a sufficient number of personnel, or great ideas if the library manager cannot persuade users to visit it. Libraries need a strong public relations program and leaders with people skills for successful implementation.

Managing library facilities, people, and programs calls for the weaving together of many diverse ideas, philosophies, and personalities. Most people in the library profession solve problems, make decisions, delegate, motivate, persuade, set personal and professional goals, and deal with difficult people. People skills are a prerequisite for successful processes and outcomes, and library managers need to know and practice the necessary communication skills to be effective leaders.

References

Riggs, Donald E., and Gordon A. Sabine. 1988. *Libraries in the '90s: What the Leaders Expect.* New York: Oryx Press.

1

SUCCESSFUL
MANAGEMENT SKILLS

Many management techniques and theories formulated by profit-minded businesses and industries also apply to non-profit organizations. As library managers strive to provide information services for users of publicly supported libraries, they face management challenges similar to those found in for-profit circumstances.

Successful library management depends on knowledge, abilities, and effective implementation of people skills. This chapter reviews the role of management and discusses the personal characteristics, abilities, and skills required for success.

According to Warren Bennis and Burt Nanus, the personal qualities needed to run an organization are persistence and self-knowledge, willingness to take risks and accept losses, commitment, consistency, challenge, and perpetual learning (1985, 187-88). Persistence is the degree to which tasks begun are finished, even when they become difficult or do not receive uniform appreciation. Giving up in sports means the team loses. Giving up in the library profession means the patrons lose. A library manager demonstrates persistence when he or she takes the time necessary to pursue needed knowledge and skills.

Library managers with self-knowledge are usually aware of their competencies and their weaknesses, and that helps them run the library effectively. Awareness of gaps in personal skills and a willingness to learn and improve is important to the development of strong library management.

A willingness to take risks and accept losses is a part of the ability to create a vision. A library manager who waits for the ultimate technology before adding *any* technology to the collection is not a risk-taker and may be someone who tries to hide mistakes. Limiting staff to tried-and-true programming rather than encouraging the use of something new restricts the library users to traditional experiences in a constantly changing world. Good management encourages risk-taking and sees that everyone makes an effort to achieve success.

Successful library managers make a commitment and give the organization their best possible personal performance. They couple a belief in the worth of the organization with the zeal to protect and the skill to promote their library to the community. Staff members make their own commitment to excellence when they understand their manager's level of dedication.

Consistency may be difficult to achieve, but it is essential for effective management. Staff and library patrons expect fair and consistent treatment at all times. When making a request, the only thing more disconcerting than having to "read" whether or not it is a good or bad day for asking is not knowing the probable outcome of the request.

Daily challenges keep management fresh and vital. Library managers bring out quality performance in everyone by challenging themselves and their staff to participate in problem identification and resolution.

Ellen is the head of reference at a large medical library. She knew something was wrong when she saw the look of regret on Jann's face. As the medical library's secretary, Jann maintained the bookkeeping records on amounts encumbered and spent. Ellen based the cost of her acquisitions on Jann's recordkeeping. Unfortunately, Jann neglected to encumber a $5,000 entry on the library's spreadsheets, and the university accounting sheets now showed a deficit of $5,000 for the reference department.

Ellen faced a challenge. Jann was a valued employee, but this was a serious mistake. Ellen initially felt angry because she thought this problem might reflect poorly on her management skills. It frustrated Ellen to have no money left in the account. However, she recognized that Jann was upset, and she did not want to make the situation worse. Ellen reviewed the problem briefly with Jann and then asked for time to think about the dilemma.

After a walk around the building, Ellen cooled down and identified the true challenge. The real problem was a lack of money for future purchases, not Jann or her overall performance. They met and discussed several possibilities that would allow them to fulfill scheduled book purchases. They considered shifting monies from other reference accounts and canceling an equipment order. The equipment order could be delayed two months until the next budget year, and they decided it was the best alternative. Their working relationship grew stronger, and Ellen's management skills were strengthened.

Management is a lifelong learning process. There are always new management techniques, new methods of administration, new ways to deal with the effects of varying trends and complex issues in the library environment, and new technologies for meeting the needs of library staff and patrons. Perpetual learning is necessary for management and staff alike, but the job of encouragement for such pursuits falls mainly to management. People with the qualities outlined above should be well positioned to fulfill a role in management.

Managers are not just managers. They often fulfill many roles. Typical job descriptions include:

Manager. Responsible for organizational planning, including developing a mission statement, setting goals, and creating a strategic plan. Provides or facilitates decision making, motivating, team building, delegating, problem solving, listening, and communications to empower staff and move the library into a priority position within the community it serves.

Supervisor. Hires, fires, trains, directs, rewards, promotes, suggests improvements, guides, and motivates staff.

Liaison. Establishes and maintains relationships with people outside the organization in business, industry, and the community as a whole. Attends social events and conferences and serves on boards, committees, clubs, and associations. Serves also as *institutional representative*, presiding over meetings and ceremonial events, representing the organization in a variety of situations, and using social functions to promote the library and its mission. Becomes a *disseminator*, communicating information gathered from meetings, conferences, reports, and memos to those who need the information.

Leader. Responsible for leadership within the organization. According to Bennis and Nanus, "leadership is the pivotal force behind successful organizations and that to create vital and viable organizations, leadership is necessary to help organizations develop a new vision of what they can be, then mobilize the organization change toward the new vision" (Bennis and Nanus 1985, 2-3).

The Role of Manager

Developing the Mission Statement

The role of a library manager includes developing and refining the library's mission statement, a formalized declaration of the fundamental reasons for the library's existence. The mission statement establishes the scope of library activities and provides overall direction by acting as the foundation for development of general and specific goals that will set the parameters for program planning. Be it general or specific, current or futuristic, the mission statement should consider the needs of the clientele. A mission statement is the first component to review or develop for an organization.

This mission statement from the American Library Association, as accepted by the ALA Council, is a good example:

> The mission of the American Library Association is to provide leadership for the development, promotion, and improvement of library and information services and the profession of librarianship to enhance learning and ensure access to information for all. (ALA 1995, 2)

Planning

The role of manager includes organizational planning—looking to the future to determine those developments that will affect the library. Managers usually accomplish organizational planning along with development of a long-range plan. While it's true that the environmental changes for many libraries are so rapid that a "long-range" plan might be obsolete in three months, no organization can function effectively without a plan. Many businesses turn to strategic planning, which, Tracey tells us

> is not the same as long-range planning. Long-range planning is concerned with a forecast of where a company's sales and

profits *might* be in ten or twenty years. Strategic planning is concerned with identifying the *most likely* issues, opportunities, challenges, and options over a shorter period. (Tracey 1990, 36)

In a workshop at an American Library Association conference in 1986, Glen H. Tecker, who served as a consultant to ALA during its strategic planning, listed five characteristics for successful planning in voluntary organizations. They are equally applicable to the library in a non-profit environment.

- The process of planning is as important as the products of planning.

- Planning is highly participative.

- All interested parties participate in planning as partners.

- The products of planning (reports and documents) are clear, concise, and easy to read.

- Long-range planning is linked to annual planning and evaluation.

First, the process of planning is as important as the resulting plan. This concept may be new to some, but it is logical. The recognition of the importance of the planning process introduces one new management technique, Total Quality Management (TQM). TQM uses a wide variety of people in the planning process, confirming that the process is at least as important as the product because it includes those affected by the plan in the planning process.

Further, TQM echoes the participation facet of the second and third criteria of Tecker's successful planning and adds a new dimension—quality. TQM is a 14-point process designed to relate effective management to strategic planning while advocating attention to quality. A library manager encourages his or her staff to make a commitment for personal quality and accountability.

An effective library manager with good TQM skills concentrates on involving everyone in maintaining and expanding the quality of all library operations.

For further reading on this topic, see Rosanna M. O'Neill's *Total Quality Management in Libraries* (Englewood, CO: Libraries Unlimited, 1994).

The fourth criterion of Tecker's strategic planning is that final documents be clear, concise, and easy to read. The audience who reads the plan includes many non-librarians. For the entire audience to understand the content, managers must write planning documents free of jargon and acronyms. The first product in the strategic plan is the mission statement, and it must be clear, concise, and easy to read.

Finally, the strategic plan must become part of the overall plan for the library. All other aspects of library operations must consider the strategic plan and take it into account for all long-range and annual plans, budgeting constraints, staff development and evaluations, and goals (or mission statement) of the library.

Preparing the Strategic Plan

The strategic plan starts once the mission statement is in place. Tracey gives some considerations for this process.

> The success or failure of any business today is not decided solely by its resources or by the conditions under which it operates, but rather by the ability of its manager to match the two. And that is what strategic planning is all about. . . . Strategic planning represents a commitment to the future of the organization rather than just letting things happen. (Tracey 1990, 35)

For a planning process to result in an effective outcome, there are two primary considerations. First, someone must develop an outline of the process for development of the plan, including measurable milestones. Second, administrators and staff must be willing to participate in the process at all times. After these two considerations, proceed with the following steps.

1. Conduct a needs assessment and analyze the data collected. Determine how far the library is from meeting the mission statement for the organization. The library may hire someone to conduct a needs assessment to see if the staff and library community perceive that the programs, services, and collection are meeting user needs at the level perceived by management.

2. Identify a direction and destination for the organization. Because strategic plans begin with the goals of the organization, organizations make decisions for meeting long-term results that improve the library and its operations. What will the library become in the immediate future? What about the next five years? Think about the economic situation of the future. Project future demands for current programs and requirements for new programs.

Decide who and how many people to include in this decision. When using the TQM model, a manager involves most of the staff and includes users and other members of the library community in preliminary planning for the direction of new services. Using Tecker's recommendations, include more staff rather than fewer staff in the decision-making process.

3. Identify needed changes. Prioritize them from the greatest to the lowest priority.

4. Establish short- and long-range goals based on the mission statement. According to Tracey, "strategic plans are built on a foundation of the organization's goals, which are statements of desired long-term results, expressed as improvements—how much and in what direction" (1990, 37). Writing well-designed goals makes it easier to plan for implementation of the strategies. It also provides a better framework for evaluation techniques.

Once the goals have been identified, the next step is to determine how these goals can be accomplished. Should the plan specify current methods or development of new ones?

5. Determine activities and resources needed to meet the goals. Identify necessary resources. Consider fiscal considerations when naming the quantity and quality of staff, the equipment, and the materials. Will the library need to purchase resources or lease them? How soon will the library need to update these resources?

Personnel are among the needed resources, and they are often the most costly. A library manager needs to determine quantities and qualifications for people. What support staff is necessary to implement new technologies? Is there a need to train or retrain staff? Is there a need to acquire or change any behaviors? To whom is each person responsible and accountable? Who is responsible for each aspect of the plan? Are people accountable? Is each step clearly communicated?

Finally, make a decision about the location of all these activities. Where are the tasks performed? Is additional space needed for any of the activities?

6. Outline fiscal considerations. The budget needed to implement the various facets of the plan must contain enough detail that those reading the strategic plan get an accurate concept of the financial obligations for each segment.

7. Establish a timeline for the accomplishment of these plans. Organize a planning session, set schedules, and meet them. Management texts offer many suggestions for creating timelines, and software programs are available to display them. Creation of a timeline helps with implementation of the activities, fitting each into its own individual schedule.

8. Explain how to evaluate the plan. Throughout the planning process, everyone who participates needs some general sense of what should happen. However, there should be precise requirements to recognize when someone performs a job satisfactorily.

Conduct an evaluation of the plan at various stages along the way to facilitate changes if progress seems less than anticipated. Prior to closure, the plan should arrange for identification of both successes and those aspects that need to improve or change. Who conducts the evaluation? What criteria is used? How is data collected?

9. Determine how to present the final plan to the audience. A well-designed strategic plan should have an abstract or summary to set the stage for the full report. Make the vision clear with the mission statement and its goals. Identify resources, both those currently available and those needed for any outlined changes.

Offer a financial outline or summary in the plan, including descriptions and costs for levels of staffing, equipment and material purchases, facility and furnishings improvements, and contracted services projections.

To meet the fifth characteristic of Tecker's successful planning—that long-range planning be linked to annual planning and evaluation—repeat all of the above steps. The manager matches accomplishments against the stated needs of the library's clientele to identify progress toward meeting the goals and the mission statement.

Periodically evaluate the success of implementing changes and tasks outlined in the strategic plan. Judge the success of each task at various points along the way. John Kotter describes the following task evaluation issues as requiring "systematic attention."

- What alternatives are being considered? What tasks need to be carried out?

- Whose active participation (staff, administrators, funders, outsiders) is needed to carry out the tasks? Whose cooperation might be needed?

- Whose direct and whose covert participation or permission is necessary for the planned activities?

- What differences exist between administrators, manager, staff, and others who carry out the activities?

- What are the causes of these differences? Are they from different backgrounds or work experiences?

- Are these people likely or unlikely to want to help? Do they know how to help?

- Are they able to resist? Do they block the efforts? If so, how can resistance be overcome, training be given, or information shared? (1985, 172-74)

These management tasks are all part of supervising personnel.

The Role of Supervisor

A supervisor's duties include hiring, firing, training, guiding and coaching (suggesting improvements), rewarding, promoting, and motivating staff. To manage people effectively, supervisors must establish personal goals and help their staff develop goals.

Goals must be specific (what, when, how measured); consistent (match the goals of the organization); reasonable or realistic; and challenging. State personal goals as positively as possible, for example, "I will become an effective presenter." Follow this goal with actions to implement it, for example, "I will become an effective speaker by joining a Toastmaster's Club."

A timetable is important and should include a date for accomplishing the goal. Some goals need specific dates and times. Others are best accomplished on a continuing basis, for example, "I will become an effective speaker by joining Toastmaster's and will continue until I am satisfied with my expectations." Chances are best to accomplish a goal if it is expressed in written form, with progress checked every month or two.

There are many advantages to setting personal goals.

- When individuals set their own goals, they pursue activities on their own and take ownership more quickly than if someone sets the goals for them.

- Goal setting gives a library manager a more concrete way of measuring performance.

- Goal setting can make a job more rewarding.

- Agreed-upon goals can bring an organization together and give it direction.

- Goal setting, like planning, can prevent a crisis.

- Effective goal setting can significantly help solve interpersonal problems in an organization.

Employees match career goals to the mission statement of the library. A career goal might be, "I will increase my technology skills by attending six two-day training sessions that are offered by the Regional Library Network within the next six months."

Successful library managers understand how to help employees accomplish their personal goals and the library mission and goals. Managers act as the catalyst for achieving these aims by

- Making sure everyone understands the mission statement and consulting them regularly. This produces a constancy of purpose.

- Continuing to build and pursue quality service. This is an on-going process. Produce charts to illustrate results.

- Remembering that it is not wise to sacrifice quality for price. Qualified and educated personnel are essential.

- Defining job duties clearly and providing the support needed to fulfill them. Successful managers trust the staff to meet requirements and perform quality work. Staff members who design their projects and have authority to carry them out as they see best are able to evaluate their progress using criteria agreed on by them and the library manager. They also have pride in their work and demonstrate responsibility for the organization.

When working with staff members, a library manager should try to eliminate roadblocks and pitfalls to each staff member's assignments and provide tangible reward for the goals attained. Rewards can range from a personal, verbal recognition of a job well done to a pay raise, public recognition, or a promotion. A library manager should increase the opportunities for personal satisfaction and provide incentives for improved coaching, guidance, and performance.

Once management establishes personal and career goals, they address responsibilities for managing personnel.

Hiring. Choosing staff is a major responsibility for any manager. The level of involvement in the actual hiring has to do with the size of the organization and the "rules" for that agency. That is, public libraries and school districts may have legal regulations outlining hiring practices. The manager understands the rules and sees that regulations are met. In a less formal situation, reading application letters and interviewing applicants offers an opportunity to assess how well the new hire matches the skills of others already working in the library and how well the new hire fills a need for a special expertise. This process should determine what level of mentoring and how much orientation to the library may be needed before the new hire can work independently.

Firing. "Firing" has two categories—gentle and necessary. Gentle firing occurs when a staff member prefers to work in a setting with a different mission. One example is a person who, in spite of all opportunities, steadfastly refuses to acknowledge the existence of technology. While it is preferable for managers to choose their own employees, in most cases staff is in place when a library assigns a manager. Because it is important to have confidence in staff members, managers make immediate plans to accomplish change. When employees are unsuitable, one option is to try to help them find new positions. If a library is large enough, this may mean a transfer within the agency. If not, removal may be the only solution. A manager can write a recommendation that provides an honest appraisal of the individual's good qualities and emphasizes attributes and talents that would fit into the job sought. Because a manager is responsible for staff performance, he or she must exercise good judgment in recognizing any staff member's knowledge and skills. In building a team, it is important at all times to have confidence in all staff members.

Training. New hires and veteran staff continue to need opportunities to increase their knowledge and skills. Staff in larger libraries may have opportunities for in-house staff development programs, while managers of smaller staffs may send them to outside workshops and conferences. The effective manager builds such programs into the budget to keep staff abreast of innovation and change.

Guiding and Coaching. The successful manager guides and coaches staff rather than expecting the staff to follow orders blindly. A good coach gets the best performance from individuals by making sure they have the necessary expertise. If not, they receive training. Staff members must understand the expectations, and they must receive rewards when they achieve them.

Rewarding. Rewarding staff can be as simple as a smile and "thank you," or it can take the form of increases in salary or recognition at an awards event. Staff needs to be aware of the reward structure and how management acknowledges performance.

George worked as a custodian in the district media center. Kit, the director of the center, observed George's ability to "fix" things and asked about his background in technology. She learned that George wanted to use new skills he acquired after taking courses at a local technical school. Through Kit's guidance and coaching, George continued his classes and took a position as a repair technician in the center. George began coming to work in a white shirt and tie. Kit continued to provide George opportunities and encouragement, such as telling administrators how George saved the district money through his exceptional technical abilities. George's interpersonal skills continued to improve, and a salary increase was justified when they revised his job description.

Promoting. Recommending staff for promotion is the highest form of reward. Promoting recognizes superior skill and ability and implies that the manager has confidence in the staff member to accomplish additional assignments. It also indicates that this staff member can be even more successful with increased responsibilities.

Motivating. Because motivating is such an important aspect of management, chapter 3 is devoted to discussions of motivating—the gentle art of persuasion.

The Role of Liaison

The role of liaison includes representing the library at outside gatherings and disseminating information from sources outside the library to the library staff. Successful library managers establish and maintain relationships with people in the community, business, and industry. Because the atmosphere is less formal, a liaison discovers much information by talking with people while attending service organization meetings, social events, and conferences. Expanding the library's presence by participating in "service tasks," such as serving on boards, committees, clubs, and associations helps position the role of the library in the community.

It is an honor to be asked to represent an institution in the community. In this role, a library manager presides over meetings and ceremonial events, representing the organization in a variety of situations. These social functions promote the library and its mission.

After events with duties as liaison or institutional representative, a library manager communicates gathered information. Attendance records, reports, and memos from meetings and conferences are distributed to those benefiting from such information.

Personal Skills

Time Management

One critical factor in accomplishing tasks is the use of time management. There are many books and speeches on time management. An army of consultants is available to conduct workshops on this topic, and they ask tough questions such as "How quickly can you find a document on your desk top? How quickly can anyone find a document on your desk when you ask someone to find it? When you begin your day, have you decided the first and second task you need to do, and do you finish it before you leave for the day? Are you bothered by frequent interruptions that keep you from finishing tasks that require concentration?" Success comes with practice of time management techniques.

Delegate work and responsibilities. Although it may seem to take more time to explain than to do it in the first place, a task that should be delegated—but is not—takes time away from another activity that is a library manager's responsibility. See chapter 4 for a more detailed discussion.

Make "to do" lists. Put the most important tasks at the top. Keep a log, recording activities performed in 10-minute segments. Allocate time by types of activities: fixed (meeting scheduled appointments); flexible (returning phone calls, going through mail, and answering correspondence, working with students or teachers in a school situation, community groups in the public library); and variable (situations beyond personal control).

Set an agenda for meetings. Meetings with set agendas and assigned time allocations help ensure that those present pay attention to the subject of the discussion. One company has all its meetings in a room with high tables and no chairs; another has a light switch timed to turn off the lights after the length set for the meeting. People who understand that there is a set agenda and a fixed time period are more likely to focus on meaningful discussion.

Set aside specific time for answering mail, returning telephone calls, and accepting appointments. This allows the manager to focus on the task at hand such as answering mail and returning telephone calls, rather than accepting distractions and then refocusing on the initial task.

Set priorities for daily commitments. While it may be difficult to complete everything established as activities for one day, it is satisfying to recognize accomplishment of priority items. It is also important to set aside quiet time for creative work or reflection.

Avoid handling any paper more than once. Take specific action immediately. Clutter on a desk usually represents disorganized paper piles that may result in lost documents, scattered information, and untimely responses to requests.

While time management takes a lesser position in management schemes, it remains an effective tool for seeing that activities move forward to meet the strategic plan.

Howard, a library director for a large university library, employs time management in the following ways:

1) Howard's secretary divides his mail into five baskets:
External business/professional
In-house business/professional
E-mail response needed
Junk
Personal

He and his secretary respond to his mail first thing in the morning and before the staff has arrived.

2) Howard carries his daily schedule on a pocket personal data assistant that "beeps" him 30 minutes before a scheduled appointment.

Minimizing Stress

To perform effectively and maintain a positive outlook, it is necessary to minimize the stress that can deplete energy and reduce effectiveness. The following suggestions may help develop a reasonable control of health and well-being.

- Do not waste time worrying about what you cannot control.

- Concentrate on what is within your control by choosing your responses to events.

- Take care of problems at the time they develop.

- Be positive.

- Develop the ability to say "no" to unimportant or low priority activities.

- Develop the philosophy of being satisfied with having done your best.

- When possible, seek the jobs that you enjoy.

- Maintain good health habits, including getting enough sleep.

- Devote time to an interest or hobby unrelated to your job.

- Keep your sense of humor and do not take yourself too seriously.

This chapter focused on successful management skills. The chapters that follow cover power, motivation and persuasion, team building, problem solving, and conflict management. The final chapter presents effective leadership skills.

References

ALA Handbook of Organization 1995/1996. 1995. Chicago: American Library Association.

Bennis, Warren, and Burt Nanus. 1985. *Leaders: The Strategies for Taking Charge.* New York: Harper & Row.

Kotter, John P. 1985. *Power and Influence.* New York: Free Press.

O'Neill, Rosanna M. 1994. *Total Quality Management in Libraries.* Englewood, CO: Libraries Unlimited.

Tecker, Glen H. June 27, 1986. Pre-Conference Workshop at an American Library Association conference.

Tracey, William R. 1990. *Leadership Skills: Standout Performance for Human Resources Managers.* New York: AMACOM.

2

TYPES AND SOURCES
OF POWER

Library managers need power to fulfill a long list of responsibilities. In particular, they need power to motivate staff to accomplish goals that support the manager's vision and the library's statement of mission. Library managers need to understand the types and sources of power and various methods of increasing their own power. An effective manager learns to use power wisely for the benefit of personal and organizational objectives. The power discussed in this chapter is a positive force used to benefit others.

Power Relationships

According to Kouzes and Posner, "Power is an expandable pie" (1988, 162). Those who treat power as a "fixed sum," fearing that if someone has more, they will have less, are mistaken. Giving away power allows a library manager and staff member to influence each other.

Power generates four outcomes: win-lose, lose-lose, lose-win, and win-win. Library managers encounter all four of these power plays, but they should foster circumstances that permit a win-win solution whenever possible.

Parents frequently demonstrate the win-lose aspect of power when they use their authority to resolve conflicts. Another example of win-lose is the majority vote, a commonly suggested resolution to a problem. However, some win and some lose if there is not unanimity, and a library manager prefers a win-win solution. Carried to undesirable extremes, a library manager with a strong win-lose attitude could say, "Everybody's had their say. Those not in favor of this project may signify by saying, 'I resign.'" Exercise of power with win-lose results can be necessary and appropriate, but it is difficult to wield wisely.

A lose-lose solution is not consensus, but compromise. Each group gives up a little to get the other group to accept the outcome.

Most labor unions foster lose-lose in their negotiations. In the case of striking librarians in public libraries and schools districts, arbitration becomes a lose-lose process. The public becomes disenchanted with disruption, and the board of directors and the public library staff establish an adversarial relationship. In a school library, the adversarial relationship may exist among the school board, superintendent, and principals with their teaching staffs, including school library media specialists.

Lose-win is the "don't rock the boat" syndrome. At its worst, it represents retreat; at its best, appeasement. A library manager who refuses to deal with a problem or face a necessary confrontation loses, and the people whose motives are destructive to the group or organization as a whole win. Ignoring issues leaves them smoldering to flame up at inopportune moments. A library manager who consistently chooses a lose-win solution is someone with dwindling power and decreasing effectiveness as a leader.

Win-win solutions represent the best scenarios. A consensus approach to decision making permits everyone to have a say, think through the issues, accept suggestions and revisions, and find the ultimate win-win solution. For a win-win situation to evolve, a library manager and staff must demonstrate concern for each other, recognize the different needs and values of each member, and build up trust rather than tear down egos. Group members must recognize that their actions impinge upon the actions of others, that the activity of one member causes significant consequences for others.

A win-win philosophy where all parties work toward a positive conclusion and share ownership of the final solution is far more successful than a purely competitive approach. The solution includes noticeable concern for one another and an awareness of and interest in each other's feelings, emotions, thoughts, and attitudes. A win-win atmosphere is one where the values and ideals of each member are accepted. Each group member has a right to express an opinion and count on consideration of that opinion. Each member is entitled to present alternatives. A good library manager presents the elements necessary to choose appropriate alternates, including constraints and consequences for each position.

SOURCES OF POWER

Power—the ability to induce or influence behavior—is classified into seven categories.

personal power

associate power

power from position held

credential power

commonality power

power in granting rewards

empowerment

Personal Power

Personal power is the inner sense of power recognizable by a person's influence, attitude, and behavior. Managerial success without personal power is unlikely because it is the only kind of power that someone cannot give or take away. Personal power is in the hands of each library manager as an individual.

Personal power derives from the following characteristics: high self-esteem, a positive attitude, proactivity, integrity, warmth, humor, patience, thoughtfulness, loyalty, the ability to solve problems, the willingness to recognize achievements, enthusiasm, a talent for image building, assertiveness, and a caring attitude.

High self-esteem. People with high self-esteem who project an image of comfort with themselves hold a great deal of power. Self-confident, capable, and competent people accept themselves, build on their strengths, and do something about their weaknesses. The possession of high self-esteem allows library managers to work more effectively with those around them. High self-esteem acts as a conduit where all aspirations and goals can pass into real, achievable results.

Positive attitude. People with a positive attitude are powerful. They radiate energy and make others feel good. People respond by viewing a library manager with a positive attitude as a winner. A manager with this power exhibits enthusiasm, a willingness to learn, cheerfulness, and an easy-to-get-along-with personality. The image of this behavior brings self-assurance, a sense of confidence, and high self-esteem. A positive attitudes makes a person more alert to opportunities and influences personal and professional decisions. Develop a positive attitude in the following ways:

- Smile. Make a real effort to look pleasant and interested.

- Say something positive. Give a compliment or make a positive statement.

- Change negatives to positives. Instead of saying something negative, change it immediately to something positive. For example, if a staff member is the subject of a complaint, find something positive about that person. Remarkably, this tip improves relations with everyone, not just with the staff member in question.

- Change a negative situation into an opportunity for growth. For example, when a staff member continually brags about something that makes others uncomfortable, respond to the boast by saying, without sarcasm, "This must give you confidence to undertake more risk-taking situations." Then, find a challenge for that person.

Proactivity. Take positive action to prevent problems before they arise and create new situations. For example, when funds are tight, local and state governments look at libraries as a way to reduce spending. A proactive manager works to eliminate this by writing articles in local newspapers regularly to keep the public informed of the relationship of tax dollars to services offered to the community. Improved public attitudes toward funding for libraries can result in the passage of bonds to fund libraries. A proactive library manager demonstrates real power when he or she motivates the public to support libraries.

Proactive library managers are independent people who demonstrate a high level of responsibility for themselves and their own lives. Proactive management involves choosing how to respond to events rather than following someone else's agenda. Choosing how to respond gives control and reinforces a sense of inner power.

Integrity. Library managers gain respect from others and foster self-respect by keeping commitments, being direct, and treating everyone by the same standards. Commanding respect and maintaining a high level of self-esteem are intangible yet effective sources of power.

Warmth. Library managers who demonstrate warmth in their management style foster effective communications as they put others at ease. They act naturally and convey interest in the comfort of others.

Humor. Humor prevents library managers from taking themselves too seriously. A good sense of humor increases the capacity to cope with difficult situations. When mistakes occur, find the humor and share it with others.

Patience. Patience gives a subtle kind of power that helps a library manager maintain control of a situation instead of being controlled by it. This kind of personal power, though often overlooked, is tremendously influential. A library manager who persistently pursues all the necessary steps to get a task finished, such as following through on a legislative agenda, has power of patience.

Thoughtfulness. A library manager can show thoughtfulness in many ways. Write thank-you notes, remember birthdays, congratulate others on accomplishments, and acknowledge hospital stays. Take time to write recommendations. Acknowledge superior performances on a face-to-face basis.

Another way of showing thoughtfulness is to practice finding subjects that are especially important to staff and others. Open conversations with an inquiry about children, a favorite hobby, or a recent event. People like to share things that are important to them, and a library manager's expressed concern and interest helps others feel comfortable and accepted.

Loyalty. Build loyalty among the staff members, patrons, and overall community by demonstrating personal loyalty. Don't countermand decisions and choices when responsibility has been delegated to others. Assume the best from the library staff and the patrons. Be honest and open with all levels of information that can be shared. When staff members know a library manager is trustworthy, forthright, and supportive, they will reciprocate with loyalty to the library and its management.

Ability to solve problems. Good library managers find ways to solve problems, not make problems. They offer at least one solution whenever they identify a problem. They ask staff and even library patrons to propose other solutions. For example, if a patron insists on disregarding a library policy, present the problem to the individual and ask for some ideas about how to solve it. Express what is possible and what is not. Try for a solution where everyone wins and the patron feels good about the conversation and the solution.

Recognizing achievements. People are universally gratified by recognition for achievement from a wide audience. An effective library manager strives for respected awards and honors, and supports staff members in their efforts to earn recognition—both inside and outside the library. Library managers are responsible for identifying opportunities to honor staff, such as acknowledgment for years of service. A library manager who bestows achievement awards adds to his or her power base.

Enthusiasm. Showing interest in and enthusiasm about work bestows a power that opens doors. When library managers display enthusiasm by tone of voice, they invite positive responses. A climate of high morale and inspiration is fostered for staff and patrons.

Talent for image building. Effective library managers have strong image-building skills. Images are built from actions, not words. Library managers are not born with this talent. They work hard to integrate many management techniques that build good images.

For the past decade, members of the information professional associations demanded that their associations "do something about the library's image," usually forgetting that their own actions as library professionals built images daily in the minds of users and supporters of libraries. No professional association has sufficient funds to buy enough billboards to wipe out the image of an uncaring staff member who doesn't appear willing to help or who doesn't remain with patrons long enough to help them solve their problems.

A library manager's image sets an example, projecting personal competence and lending credibility to the institution's competence. Image includes dress, communication style, the staff, and the library as a facility.

A library manager enhances his or her image of power by wearing appropriate attire although the fashion community often changes the rules for the power outfit—different colors, different styles. One professor who teaches behavior and communication skills remarked that it doesn't matter what you say when making a presentation, it's how you look while you're saying it. While this may seem simplistic, the community acquires their own perception of professional images for a library manager and the supporting staff members. Images are unmistakably influential, and an effective library manager does not disregard the potential of this power.

Another strong image-building skill exhibited by effective library managers is the creation of a communication style that projects confidence. The style may favor written or spoken communications. Sloppy letters in response to inquiries project a lack of care in other parts of the institution. Beginning oral communication with a genuine smile makes staff and patrons feel comfortable and willing to listen to the words that follow. Speaking with clear diction, and always using good English help foster good communications and build confidence.

The manner of the staff toward patrons also sets an image for the library. If staff is too "busy" to be helpful when someone approaches them, patrons will go elsewhere to meet their information needs. One bookstore employee who was enrolled in a master of library science degree program lamented the fact that so many people called the store to get "in print" information about books and titles of books on particular subjects. When the employee suggested the caller contact the public library, the retort was often, "Why?"

Often, library staff members wonder about the creation of an image for information professionals. What's important is that they must remember that they *are* the library to all of the patrons. If there is to be a change in the image of the library, it is the responsibility of every person employed in the library to improve the image, remembering that they may have to overcome some patrons' previous negative experiences.

The image of the physical facility and the collection of resources influences how the community reacts to the library. Members of the library community make decisions about funding, use of the collection, and volunteering based on their image of the library. They base decisions concerning the worthiness of the library on the display of materials and the general appearance of the physical layout. Money is well spent on paint, landscaping, and attractive and useful directional signs and layouts. Library managers should create a welcoming atmosphere with adequate space and lighting. Good lighting has the effect of a soft, complete glow rather than bright spots of lights with dark shadows in other areas. Color also plays a major role in a library environment because color has the power to motivate people toward particular actions. A professional consultant in this field can offer suggestions for redecorating a library.

When Susan interviewed for the elementary media center position and toured the facilities, she discovered appallingly poor conditions in basic equipment and furnishings. The unwelcome condition of the tables and chairs in the center—old folding chairs and discarded tables from a cafeteria—especially shocked her. It was a poor image to lure students into spending time there.

Susan's image-building skills impelled her to ask if she could make some changes in the seating. After the principal agreed on a minimal budget, she went to a local store and purchased a lawn table (with umbrella), chairs, and three picnic tables with benches. Once parents noted the difference in the "look" of the center, they made suggestions and offered supplies. The custodian helped put a coat of paint on the walls. Some parents brought in plants. One parent donated large floor pillows for the children to sit on. The parent association offered to help sponsor a book fair.

Assertiveness. Good library managers display assertiveness. Janette S. Caputo (1984, 3) provides many suggestions on how to be assertive in the work environment.

Assertive communication skills allow managers to interact with others in a positive, open, and thoughtful manner and, at the same time, model correct assertive behavior for staff members. The benefits received from enhanced interpersonal relationships include a more effective and efficient working environment with reduced stress. Library managers need to practice assertive behavior and encourage others to respond in a like manner: The following paragraphs review assertiveness in a positive way.

1. Use the pronoun "I" in statements more often than "you." This reduces the chance of a staff member becoming defensive. For example, saying, "I feel worried about you . . ." instead of "You should not . . . ," may make the other person more receptive as it takes the focus and pressure off them.

2. Be honest and sincere. From early childhood, individuals learn to recognize insincerity, although it is sometimes more difficult to analyze honesty in a brief encounter. To paraphrase President Lincoln, one can fool some of the staff some of the time, but it is impossible to fool all of the staff all of the time. They quickly learn when their manager is insincere or dishonest, and their behavior will reflect this.

3. Recognize the importance of appropriate and immediate responses to unusual situations. If a staff member continues a lengthy telephone conversation after a patron approaches the reference desk, a library manager needs to remind the desk staff that there is a policy of acknowledging patrons immediately. Practice saying something to express feelings at the time they occur, such as, "It is unfortunate that some patrons think that we do not respond to their requests as quickly as possible. Let's always acknowledge their presence even while we're answering a telephone reference question." If the discussion is delayed until a later staff meeting, the staff members

might misunderstand and consider it a complaint against them all when, in fact, only one person had erred.

4. Avoid using speech phrases and styles that indicate tentativeness or indecisiveness, such as "maybe," "I guess," or ending a sentence with a question. While there are times when it is appropriate to express flexibility, staff should not confuse the intent of a library manager's assertion. In the previous situation where a patron was not acknowledged at the desk, a weak phrase such as "Maybe we should acknowledge their presence" would be ineffective and inappropriate. There should be no flexibility in prompt acknowledgment of a patron. The flexibility of options for staff at the desk would occur after the patron has been acknowledged. The staff member could volunteer to call the telephone patron back after locating the information while making eye contact with the in-house patron and promising attention as soon as possible. Another option would be to request the aid of another librarian and make sure the in-house patron recognized that help was on its way.

5. Say "no" to unreasonable requests without feeling guilty. Librarians who are trained to respond to the needs of others may find it difficult to say "no" to anyone. After all, library work is a service profession. However, a library manager must place limits on repeated and possibly unreasonable requests placed on one staff member to avoid the appearance of favoritism. In granting any request, the astute library manager also considers the future. If an "unreasonable" request is honored, it may set a precedent for others to ask the same or similar requests. When a library manager considers such future possibilities, it is easier to change a feeling of guilt into a healthy perspective of necessary management.

6. Speak in a clear, audible voice without rushing. Use brief pauses. People who talk rapidly are more difficult to understand because the listener has little time to interpret what is said or translate it into an expected action.

7. Use eye contact whenever appropriate, but be aware that this is a culturally biased action because in some cultures eye contact is a negative. The manager should not consider the inability of a staff member to make eye contact as an indication of guilt; it may represent respect.

8. Make common, straightforward statements of needs with courtesy and thoughtfulness. For example, ask a staff member to "Please send this message to Alice."

9. Share anger without aggression or accusation. Speak without flagrant emotion, and use "I" statements. "I feel great disappointment in the way you treated our custodian." "Perhaps I could provide better service if you exhibited more courtesy."

10. Resolve problems created by a previous agreement. Restate the problem, find out where the difficulty lies, and renegotiate or reaffirm the agreement. For example, "I thought we agreed to respond immediately when patrons came to the reference desk. Why did you not greet the patron?"

11. Admit mistakes and express intention to correct them. For example, it is better to say, "It's true I asked you to write a memo that conflicts with previous instructions. I'm sorry I wasn't more consistent. I'll write an apology and reword the memo."

12. Choose to postpone when a response is "inconvenient." It is sometimes inconvenient, for example, to give a lengthy defense or explanation when an angry patron blames a library staff member for a policy dictated by the board of directors. For example, the operating hours might change because reduced funding required a cut in library hours. A library manager should avoid negative assertiveness such as blaming the patron (or the community as a whole) for reduced funding levels. Instead, the manager might display positive assertiveness by sympathizing with the patron and suggesting the patron write a letter to the board of directors.

A caring attitude. Managers in libraries must care about others and show that they care. Library management is a service profession, and a dictatorship is not appropriate. Recognize the feelings of others. When asking a staff member to take a message to Alice, say, "I know you are trying to finish the inventory, but I'd really appreciate it if you could deliver that message to Alice now." Express emotions toward others in a thoughtful and sincere manner. Staff members who do their jobs well, give assistance to patrons, or receive acknowledgment from a professional association should hear "You make us all look good" from management.

Actively listen by making eye contact, leaning forward, and nodding at appropriate comments. At the end of a conversation, ask for time to research the matter and tell the patron to expect a response by a specified time.

Personal power is one of the most important assets of a successful library manager. It requires all of the above characteristics, but its true strength comes from a caring attitude. Managers who show an honest interest in their staff members both on and off the job, who make an effort to be visible to all, and who work to see that people are given an opportunity to achieve their highest potential will succeed. Their team will be motivated to work hard to meet the mission of the library, overcoming incredible obstacles by focusing efforts on the mission. A caring library manager helps make staff look good, and when the a staff look good, the manager looks good, too.

Position Power

Position power is exercised within the parameters of the job description. This is perhaps the weakest and most unreliable type of power because title and job description are not stable over long periods of time.

People who apply for management positions should assess very carefully the actual power of the job. If the job is merely a title without associated management power and authority, it may not be a job worth pursuing. The new manager might need to devote a tremendous amount of effort into building up position power in the absence of a strong job description.

A library manager can achieve position power by understanding the job description, satisfying the expectations of those responsible for hiring and firing, and fulfilling each element of the job description with a high degree of performance. To obtain position power, the manager must gain the confidence and trust of those responsible for deciding the limits of a manager's power. The best library managers develop a reputation for meeting the expectations of the job description with dependability and trustworthiness.

Sid, a high school library manager, finished preparing a technology grant proposal four days before the deadline. Prior to submission, however, it required approval from the school board and the school district superintendent. Unfortunately, the school board was not due to meet for five days. Sid requested an extension from the grantee committee, and he also called the school district's superintendent's secretary, Alice, for assistance. She agreed to talk to the superintendent.

The following day, the grantee committee turned down Sid's request for an extension, but Alice had good news for him. The school superintendent agreed to sign the proposal before the grantee committee met because he knew Sid to be a responsible, respected, and successful library manager. Sid's position power enabled him to overcome an obstacle to his grant submission. Later, the school board approved the technology grant.

Another method of gaining additional power is to get it written into an updated job description. A library manager needs the responsibility of staff selection to ensure that those hired match the perceived needs of the manager. In public libraries and school districts, politics or legalities may dictate what happens in hiring. The governing board may use its ability to appoint staff as a perk, meaning that their friends are placed in staff positions without benefit of a competency and compatibility assessment. Seniority policies may give preference to existing staff over someone more qualified from outside the system. If responsibility for hiring guidelines can be shifted through a change in a library manager's job description, the manager's position acquires a great deal more power.

People also gain position power by assuming responsibility for special resources or information. Serving as a special resource person to an important committee or organization puts the manager in the center of the action and provides useful information. When people recognize a library manager as someone who provides information that helps the group make better decisions, they subtly shift power to the library manager.

In a public library environment, providing information to city officials who make decisions improves the image of the library and enhances a library manager's position power. In a school district situation, power grows when a library manager helps district administrators gain a higher regard for the school by offering them information to improve curriculum and, providing them an up-to-date analysis of successful programs in other districts across the nation. One library manager prepared a database of the state's school laws, legal interpretations, and implementation record.

Use position power as a positive tool to influence others. Share information among all interested parties, including other administrators, funding agencies, and the library staff. Disseminate information as expeditiously as possible. Try to anticipate needs, for information and knowledge are sources to enhance the position power of a library manager.

Associate Power

Associate power is derived from other professionals. Examples of associate power sources include mentors, influential people, and allies.

Mentors. Brooke Sheldon suggests that the good managers should mentor staff members. However, most new managers need to be students before they become mentors.

> Increasingly, in all professions, there is a growing awareness that the presence of mentors and role models can be a critical factor in one's career.... Leaders spot and seek out potential leaders, but they also understand that part of their role is to encourage mentees to move off in their own directions. (Sheldon 1991, 51)

Sheldon gives examples of leaders as mentors "pulling people along, demanding the best, and providing opportunities both on the job and in professional organizations" (1991, 51). An influential person is an especially helpful mentor in many ways, such as providing introductions to others in power positions. Choose a mentor with enviable qualities, but also consider the mutual impact of a long and close association. While most people feel complimented when chosen as a mentor, a library manager needs to confirm whether the person is available and has the time for mentoring, especially if the candidate mentor is an influential person. For successful mentoring, the mentor must be available to a library manager on a frequent basis.

Library managers must remember that other individuals also seek mentors, and as they acquire experience and power, they should make themselves available as mentors to others.

Influential people. Getting to know important people helps a library manager network and enhance his or her power base. Managers who hold positions in their home community interact with respected and influential people they already know. To reinforce a base of power, list key people in local and regional organizations, including service (Kiwanis), social (university alumni groups), professional (local librarians), and community (political party affiliation). Contact three people on the list each week to maintain a professional relationship with potential benefits for the manager and the library organization. Ask a mentor to expand the list.

People do business with people they know. Be a respected leader in the community and the library profession, and serve on committees that benefit the library. Be sure people know about librarians and the work they do. For example, joining a service organization such as Rotary and volunteering to serve on committees expands a library manager's list of influential people. Write articles for magazines, journals, or newspapers. Join career associations or groups and read relevant publications. Establish a network of people to support the library.

Allies. Having allies enhances influence. When library managers need information quickly, they may use allies to obtain it. If a crisis in city government places the library funding in jeopardy, allies provide early warning and subsequent support for the library and associated issues.

Credential Power

Credential power emanates from one's education, experience, or accomplishments and dictates whether an individual meets the criteria outlined in the job description. Acquisition of credential power is within the control of each individual.

People wishing to move into library management or into more responsible management positions should set goals to obtain the necessary experience or education required for the career move. They may need additional education for new technologies. In a public library, the person may need a master's degree from a program accredited by the American Library Association. In a school library, they may need an administrator's certification.

Credential power also accrues to managers who update their skills. New methods of management in business soon find their way into libraries. Chapter 1 discussed total quality management (TQM) as one method that transcended commercial business and found a place in library management. It's focus on meeting the needs of internal and external customers translates perfectly well to library management working to understand and meet the needs of staff and patrons. Vocabulary is not a problem when reviewing literature for potential application to library environments. "Downsizing" in business, for example, is simply "restructuring" in a school setting. Remaining aware of business trends helps a library manager predict the next management trend for the library.

Managers help their staff maintain and improve credential power. Allowing staff time off to attend workshops and classes for credit will add to their skills and improve library services. A manager in a small public library in rural Pennsylvania "grew" a highly competent staff by encouraging paraprofessional workers to expand their skills by attending a nearby university program with a master of library science program.

Commonality Power

Commonality power is recognizing or developing a manager's similarities or commonalties with others. Effective library managers belong to social clubs, professional societies, athletic organizations, or performing arts groups to maintain a network of people who share specific interests and values. Commonality power enhances personal careers and provides support for library goals.

Building commonality through shared interests and values increases power even more when managers draw as many others as possible into the library network. Helping staff establish networks also strengthens the library program and develops additional allies.

Reward Power

The power to grant internal or external awards gives great satisfaction to library managers. In 1943, Abraham Mazlow described a hierarchy of human needs and Frederick Herzberg applied these needs to the workplace in 1950. Internal rewards begin with basic needs, those that provide the opportunity for an employee to grow in their job. These offer the greatest long-term results, increasing motivation and making life at work more satisfying, for example giving staff members the opportunity to learn new things as they work. Link good performance with rewards; good job performance equals employee recognition.

It's easy to give internal rewards. Offer staff opportunities to attend workshops and conferences and encourage staff to experiment with different ways of accomplishing assigned tasks more efficiently. Involve staff members in work they enjoy and allow them to take risks, such as experimenting with new computer software to enhance productivity.

External rewards include material benefits. Although external rewards work well as incentives for motivated performance, results are usually of shorter duration than with well-developed internal rewards. Pay increases, bonuses, promotions, personal recognition, public praise, and special benefits such as a personal parking space are typical external rewards. Use reward power discretely because if administered unfairly, it lessens a library manager's power. A library manager who handles rewards effectively knows what people find rewarding and provides those rewards appropriately.

Empowerment

Empowerment means helping people reach their highest level of performance by giving them the opportunity and means to do so. Unlike other types of power—power over others—empowerment shares and delegates power. Sharing power through empowerment is the highest level of power. Involving employees in the operation of the library and sharing authority and responsibility with them empowers them and increases the manager's ability to accomplish tasks to meet goals. All successful managers empower others.

Share information. While withholding information gives a manager a certain kind of power, ultimately, it is destructive. Staff members who recognize that information is kept from them begin to withhold information from others. An open environment with shared information allows all members of the staff to see where they fit into the big picture and helps them match their tasks beneficially to others.

Hold staff members accountable for their work. Enforcing job accountability is an important part of library management. Accepting responsibility is part of a staff member's role, and they expect rewards based on their success in accepting and carrying out responsibilities. When one staff member fails to complete a task, it adversely affects whether other staff members complete their assignments. A library manager must maintain the work flow, empower staff members to do their work, and expect them to successfully complete jobs within the planned time. Managers must ensure that no obstacles exist that might hinder staff performance.

Allow people to be risk takers. Staff members who fear for their positions if they do not follow directions precisely will not consider alternative ways to accomplish a task. Fear of consequences stifles creativity and reduces opportunity for positive changes. An effective library manager encourages all staff members—from clerical to experienced professionals—to discuss and experiment with new and innovative procedures and solutions.

Allow people to make mistakes. Don't penalize staff members who are willing to experiment, to be risk takers, if their grand idea does not work the first time. Allow them to review the problem, revise their scheme, and try an alternative approach. Allowing mistakes does not forfeit control, but it means not penalizing staff members who commit errors without careful consideration. Staff members who fear severe, job-loss consequences for their mistakes expend great effort to hide errors instead of working out early, corrective solutions. Hiding errors compounds problems and makes it difficult to find solutions. Try to find honest reasons for mistakes. They may not result from simple carelessness. A staff member may need re-training or may need additional training. The activity may be boring or repetitive.

Help people to fulfill both organization and personal goals. Guide people to fulfill goals through their own initiative. They will gain a sense of accomplishment and personal power. Use power to help them—internal and external rewards, influence, empowerment.

Build a "family" atmosphere. Most staff meets a higher standard of performance when there is team spirit and a feeling of kinship with each other. It energizes everyone when they feel they are an integral part of the organization or group.

The late Sam Walton, founder of Wal-Mart, was a great proponent of staff empowerment. He built a strong corporate culture and encouraged risk taking. He knew that if he treated his employees well, the employees would treat customers the same way.

Effective library managers share power through empowerment. Sharing authority and responsibility results in a collective effect and increases the actual power of library managers. The more power a manager shares or gives, the more power he or she receives in return. For example, treating staff members as team players increases performance, boosts morale, and lessens complaints. A library manager learns that cultivating self-esteem makes it easier to share power. Managers who balance their personal needs and professional goals with those of others find their power increased.

References

Caputo, Janette S. 1984. *The Assertive Librarian.* New York: Oryx Press.

Herzberg, Frederick, Bernard Mausner, and Barbara Block Synderman. 1959. *The Motivation to Work.* 2d ed. New York: John Wiley.

Kouzes, James M., and Barry Z. Posner. 1988. *The Leadership Challenge: How to Get Extraordinary Things Done in Organizations.* San Francisco: Jossey-Bass.

Mazlow, Abraham. 1954. *Motivation and Personality.* New York: Harper & Row.

Sheldon, Brooke E. 1991. *Leaders in Libraries: Styles and Strategies for Success.* Chicago: American Library Association.

3

MOTIVATION

Successful library managers motivate their staff by understanding and building on the personal needs of employees. Whereas a traditional, directive approach often emphasizes the use of external rewards for motivation, using a participatory style of management creates opportunities for personal and professional growth. A traditional, direct management style that relies on external rewards for motivation is less successful in bringing out employees' best performance.

The participatory model of human motivation assumes that people need more than security. They also need growth and self-fulfillment. Abraham Maslow, a behavioral psychologist, first charted these needs in 1943 with his *Theory of Human Motivation* and his Hierarchy of Human Needs. His lists included physiological needs; safety, stability, security; belonging, love and social activity; self-esteem, esteem of others, status; self-realization, and fulfillment. In 1950, Frederick Herzberg in *The Motivation to Work* presented his theory of work motivation, including personal life (salary or wages, fringe benefits); working conditions (company policies and administration, work environment); interpersonal relations (supervision, peers, subordinates); status; advancement, recognition, and achievement. While some human resource experts question the validity of Herzberg's and Maslow's models, they acknowledge that the models motivate people and help them reach self-fulfillment.

Personal Life

Opportunities for improving personal life—at home and at work—are fundamental motivational factors. Employees need to obtain salary and benefits that support a rewarding personal life. Staff members need to feel adequately compensated for their work., and managers need to communicate that employees receive the best salaries and benefits available within the budget. Government agencies fund most library jobs, and staff salaries are usually public information. Count on employees making comparisons between their own compensation and that of others.

When there is a salary scale, advancement often relies on specific experience and education. This is true in most public schools and in public libraries with union wage scales or civil service ratings from the state. Salary scales may provide for annual raises, but most salary increases require staff members to learn different skills or seek promotions to different positions. In the salary management process, it is essential that each staff member understands the criteria for merit increases. When managers base salary increases on job performance, there is an increased burden to make fair and impartial judgments on staff performance.

Staff members' personal life away from work also affects the staff members' personal life in the workplace. With the passage of federal legislation that protects the position of an employee who must take extended time off to care for a family member, employers have an obligation to accommodate employees with some kinds of family responsibilities. A library manager must also provide consideration and attention for situations not covered under this legislation. This may include schedule adjustments for single parents with children and staff members taking college courses. Finding a way to satisfy needs of the staff members' personal lives gives the manager a powerful tool of motivation. When a library manager shows interest in supporting personal life issues such as paraprofessional staff working toward professional status, it represents support for everyone's advancement.

Working Conditions

Staff needs to understand that its manager cares about mental and physical comfort in the work environment. Working conditions include both the physical setting where staff is expected to work and the relevant company policies and administrators.

Physical Comfort

Staff members need to feel good about their work environment. Provide staff with well-lighted work spaces, comfortable chairs and work spaces, and as pleasant an ambiance as possible. Many people spend more waking hours at work than at home. Make their surroundings as comfortable and attractive as possible. To motivate staff members, provide them with the best equipment possible to do their job. It's amazing how motivating a simple thing as a comfortable office chair is to a staff member who spends a great deal of time at the computer. Management should also provide effective and appropriate resources for staff members. If it is more efficient to use a spreadsheet than a ledger book to keep financial records, purchase the software and train the staff to use it.

Beware of potential safety hazards and take steps to eliminate them. Old step stools, slick flooring, and ragged carpeting are dangerous to staff and patrons alike. Taking steps to abolish such dangers not only demonstrates caring and concern it also recognizes the litigious climate in the United States today.

Psychological Comfort

Try to establish a "family" atmosphere among the staff members, with each person showing care and concern for others. Staff members need to know how to make themselves feel good about their relationships with peers, subordinates, and supervisors. Encourage them to interact positively with others. Library managers set good examples by offering sincere compliments about jobs well done and exhibiting honest care and concern for staff's welfare and for the welfare of their family and friends.

Library managers must demonstrate fairness with praise and with criticism. Employees need to know that their performance will be uniformly and consistently judged, and they deserve to know possible consequences and solutions for typical problems. Managers need to supply staff with a list of appropriate steps to improve performance and a time frame or deadline for completion of the changes.

Arrange for staff to have time away from assigned tasks. In some areas, breaks away from work are guaranteed by law. Allow staff members to enjoy their time away from the job. A comfortable staff room with leisure furniture, soft lighting, and pictures on the walls enables people to retreat into a peaceful, restful environment during their breaks.

Reduce excessive stress by suggesting a coffee break or a short walk for a staff member who is unusually tense. Try to find the reason and take action to eliminate or diminish the cause if it is work-related. Library managers reduce stress in the workplace when they demonstrate understanding for personal obligations of staff, such as caring for an elderly parent or coping with an obstreperous teenager.

Kathy, the library manager for a regional library system, recognized Lil as a valuable employee, but something seemed wrong. Lil's work was not up to its usual standard, and she missed several days because of "illness." When Kathy saw Lil all alone in the staff lounge, she asked if there was a problem. Lil shared her problems, including the stress of an imminent divorce and overwhelming concern for the welfare of her three children who lacked after-school care.

Responsive to Lil's difficulties, Kathy arranged a flexible shift to accommodate the school schedule of Lil's children, thus relieving some stress in Lil's life and helping her concentrate once more on doing a good job at the library.

Promote good health by example and by encouraging exercise and regular physical examinations (especially if they are part of an employee health package). Ensure that staff has an adequate health plan that includes an opportunity for them to include dependents. Find workshops on good health and provide encouragement and opportunities for all staff to attend. If an exercise program is available during the noon break period, encourage staff to participate.

Take into consideration the effect of any policy change. Discuss policy changes with staff members before implementing them. For example, staff needs time to adjust to a new policy limiting the use of compensatory time to half-day increments when previous policy allowed them to save up and take whole days.

A feeling of security has a direct correlation to morale in the workplace. In general, employees who feel secure in their jobs feel motivated to work. Promote a feeling of security among staff.

Match job demands and staff capabilities. Allow staff members to grow in the job, but do not put them in positions where they have no chance of succeeding.

Identify job requirements and clearly communicate expectations to staff members. Thoroughly explain the job requirements, work standards, and quality issues. Provide evaluation criteria.

Provide honest and timely feedback on performance. Be specific, timely, and constructive. Set up a regular meeting time and place. Keep student assistants or volunteer parents motivated to do a good job. Discreetly correct any poor job performance.

Assure a clear relationship between pay and performance. Reward good job performance with promotions, bonuses, and public recognition.

Interpersonal Work Relations

Staff members interact continually with each other and with administrators. Effective library managers help people achieve a sense of belonging by including them in the activities, ongoing programs, and projects within the library. Managers foster a participatory environment by ensuring equitable and fair involvement of all skilled staff members in projects. As staff plans projects, suggest inclusion of appropriate-but-overlooked staff with relevant skills and knowledge. Good library managers also help employees identify and define their individual roles within the information profession.

Two frequently unrecognized factors in motivation are enthusiasm and positive attitudes. People who possess and use enthusiasm along with a positive attitude achieve much in life. They draw notice from and influence others. Enthusiasm is contagious. It is a creative force and a catalyst for action from others. Approaching challenges with a "can-do" attitude provides a jump-start on success. Ask staff members about their interests and show genuine enthusiasm for their achievements.

Cheri, a public high school library media specialist, showcases her enthusiastic talents by hosting special library events, with refreshments, twice a year. She personally invites the entire high school staff to come and review new teaching and recreational reading resources.

Cheri gives brief reviews of new acquisitions and provides suggestions on their use in the curriculum. She solicits ideas from others, introduces staff to displays of all the resources, and distributes listings of new acquisitions. Cheri offers to go to the classrooms to review or demonstrate any of the resources. Cheri's high level of enthusiasm transmits her interest in the materials to the other school staff and fosters a team atmosphere.

Help staff plan successful programs. Give them adequate planning time and sufficient funding. Nothing sustains and increases enthusiasm as much as success.

As library managers give others what they need, others give back what the manager needs. Successful library managers motivate their employees to self-actualization.

Involve staff members in goal setting and planning. Speak in terms of "we" and "our." Employees provide more support for manager when managers include them in the planning process.

Promote team decision making and problem solving. If staff members are part of the team, they more readily accept agreements and support implementation. Find acceptable ways to include staff in the process of hiring other staff members to ensure smooth working relationships. When a problem arises, guide the staff through the problem and the search for a solution.

Involve staff members in the reviewing process. Ask staff members to review their own performances and the quality of library services and programs offered. They know what works and what does not. Most people don't like to analyze their own performance because they hesitate to illuminate their weaknesses, but the process helps library managers understand staff and work toward personal and organizational improvements.

Be attentive. Make certain that employees receive sufficient attention. Be aware of how employees' day-to-day activities (including mundane tasks) contribute to the effective functioning of the library. Accept their suggestions for ways to improve their tasks.

Promote self-management. Promote self-management within the staff. Self-esteem is closely linked to feelings of freedom and control over work. Management by objectives (individual accountability for documented goals) enables them to meet and reach these objectives with minimal supervision.

Ask for ideas and opinions. When management solicits and sincerely evaluates ideas and opinions, they boost workers' self-esteem. Request ideas and help from staff when making changes and solving problems. In the spirit of TQM, encourage them to take ownership of issues. Be sure to give people credit for their ideas and contributions, making the recognition public whenever appropriate.

Recognize good work. Recognize the good work of individuals. Place any need for improvement in perspective when judging an individual's total performance, giving recognition to good work first.

Exhibit personal interest. Show a personal interest in the development of each staff member. The time it takes to build a relationship is some of the most effective and important time a library manager spends. The effort returns a highly motivated work unit.

Identify personal goals. Identify the personal goals of each staff member. What is important to them? What do they want to accomplish? What do they want to become? Do they want recognition for intelligence, performance, a caring attitude, or talent?

Provide effective on-the-job training and coaching. Knowledge of staff members' long-range goals helps a library manager provide appropriate counseling and coaching. Be a good listener. Be supportive. Be candid. Make practical suggestions. Library managers are responsible for staff carrying out jobs effectively. Training is a motivating force. If staff members understand their jobs and their opportunities, they accomplish them more effectively and efficiently.

Provide educational opportunities. Opportunities for personal growth and success motivate staff. Analyze the needs of staff members and plan the ways and means to help them grow in their jobs. Provide opportunities for formal education or training. Take advantage of opportunities that help staff members pursue goals. See chapter 9 for suggestions on planning staff workshops to teach new strategies for providing services, new technologies, and information interfaces.

Provide career planning assistance. Show staff members a genuine interest in their career development. Encourage professional development and provide assistance for career opportunities.

Lois, a library aide, is familiar with most aspects of a school library media center. She is a fast learner, shows interest in all aspects of the program, and is very good with the students. Her own children leave soon for college, and she considers giving up the library aide job for a full-time career.

Tom, a media specialist, knows that recent school district growth requires hiring of more media specialists in the immediate future. He discusses the situation with Lois and encourages her to continue her education with specialization in library information. He also introduces her to administrators responsible for future hiring of new media specialists.

Status

Staff members need to feel good about themselves and have a sense of self-worth. Give them credit for their successes and let them know their jobs are important to the functioning of the organization. Introduce staff to visitors. Explain the position of a particular staff member and point out their contribution to a recently completed project. Assure visitors they are in good hands by sharing a story of special patron help from the staff member. Staff members need to know that people appreciate them, consider them useful, and view their role as worthwhile. When possible, provide office space to staff members. An office with a desk gives a staff member a true sense of worth and importance.

Advancement, Recognition, and Achievement

Staff members need to feel that they do meaningful work. Help staff members use their professional skills. Allow staff to complete tasks to their satisfaction. Every time a library manager makes staff lives more rewarding, staff is motivated to continue doing a good job. Supporting their efforts helps instill a desire to succeed.

Library managers usually achieve higher levels of performance from staff when they give staff a chance to see the meaningful results of ideas and hard work. For example, a manager might give public recognition to someone who comes up with a creative plan on how to remodel the reference area for greater access. Appreciation expressed by the community users is a significant source of motivation that encourages development of other new ideas for meeting the library users' needs. A good manager ensures appropriate recognition of employee achievements.

Marty, a public school district library director, meets annually with all the district library media center personnel for a breakfast meeting and awards presentation. Library managers and administrators present achievement and recognition awards. The library media center personnel in one high school received the annual principal's award for the outstanding educational program in the school.

Recognition comes from rewards that may be internal or external, personal or public. Internal rewards include quietly telling staff members of work well done. If they understand the manager's expectations and the scale that determines their success, employees build personal pride in their work. Good library managers also bestow external (public) rewards, especially sincere praise in front of others. People like to hear someone say they make a difference.

In the book, *Putting the One-Minute Manager to Work* by Blanchard and Lorber (1984), the authors suggest the following ways to praise staff.

- Let employees know in advance that there will be feedback on their work performance.

- When you learn that someone has done a good job, praise that person. Put thought into how to express the praise.

- Staff members need more than the traditional encouragement of "Good," "Very good," or "Fine."

- Be very specific about what constitutes "pleasing" actions.

- Do not rely on general affirmations of the person. Include in expressions of praise the helpful impact of the person's actions on the organization and on colleagues or fellow workers.

- During the annual evaluation of staff, bring out at least one example of a significant contribution from each staff member to the program. This is a tremendously motivating practice. (To become more familiar with these rewards, see chapter 2.)

- Don't rush sincere praise. Stopping for a moment of silence helps employees recognize genuine sincerity. Encourage the individual to continue doing more of the same.

- Offer praise at the time an employee does something noteworthy. Do not wait for annual performance reviews. Praise is most beneficial when given immediately.

Help staff members develop an interest in their work. Give them responsibility for themselves and their work. Make sure employees feel they have the potential to grow within the organization. Help them set realistic goals and assume personal responsibility for the outcomes. Give them challenging tasks, plenty of positive reinforcement, and immediate feedback.

Some people work well in competitive environments. Recognize this and provide competitive opportunities, but make sure staff understands that being the loser in the competition carries no penalty. Attendance is one kind of competition. Another is customer service. Provide an award for best treatment of users—friendly greetings and good service.

A skillful manager enables staff members to use their abilities, energy, and resources to the fullest. For example, assign staff members who are good at working with people to positions that work directly with patrons. Assign people who like computers to the interlibrary loan request desk. Whenever possible, respond to the essential interests and values of individual employees and find out what stimulates strong reactions. Identify staff members' preferences by asking them direct questions.

What do you like most about your job?

What do you like least about your job?

What would you like to do in the future?

What would you like to learn?

When do you feel you do your best work?

With whom do you prefer to work?

What is most important to you in your job?

Match likes and dislikes to present job descriptions. Is there some way to switch tasks and duties among members of the staff to allow them to do more of what they like to do most? Is it possible for them to take workshops or other means of education to help them learn what they would like to learn? Motivation is stimulated when staff knows that management asks such questions, but reallocating tasks to make jobs more appealing is an even greater motivation.

Principles of Everyday Persuasion

One form of motivation is persuasion, and an effective library manager uses it to win others to his or her own way of thinking.

Using the participatory model of motivation, the key to persuasion is leading others to fulfill their needs. Successful library managers practice persuasion techniques.

Begin a conversation with a sincere smile. Successful salespersons do not greet customers with a frown and a negative attitude. In the same way, successful library managers who wish to get their members of their staff to think differently must make the process pleasant from the start to avoid a negative atmosphere.

Get the other person to agree with you early. Get people to agree on something at the beginning of a conversation. If nothing else, agree on the weather.

Guide thinking. Understand the other person's position and use that as the basis for discussion. Persuasive library managers thoroughly explain the exact need and point out its benefit to others.

Appeal to emotions. Persuasion relies on helping people meet their emotional needs. The intensity of an individual's emotions varies, and each person handles emotions differently. Persuasive library managers tune into an individual's feelings and get on the same wavelength. When the manager learns to do this effortlessly, he or she has mastered the skill of persuasion.

Be sympathetic. A library manager must be empathetic and sympathetic to the reaction of others when trying to win them over to another way of thinking. Library managers must make sure people know they care about feelings; otherwise, people rebel instead of following the suggested change in thinking.

Appeal to the greater good. Persuasive library managers evoke the good of the community, the school district, and the life of the library user to win others to a different way of thinking. It is far easier to refuse a request from a manager than it is to turn down the needs of the library patrons. Work to show priority for students in school libraries and patrons at a public libraries.

Use testimonials. Testimonials of success are always good beginning steps to convince others to try a proposed solution. Have someone with a familiar face give the testimonial, especially to an audience with first-hand knowledge of the situation.

Ask questions simply and directly. Question others in a way that is likely to get a favorable answer. For example, if a library manager wants an administrator to provide additional travel funds for staff to attend a workshop or conference, he or she should briefly detail the benefits to the library and then simply ask for payment of travel and registration fees.

Avoid being dogmatic and argumentative. State the premise and then allow discussion. If there is little apparent basis for a negative reaction, restate the premise and invite further discussion.

Do more listening than talking. People appreciate the opportunity to be heard. An effective library manager listens to opinions and allows others to react to suggestions.

Show respect for other's opinions. It is essential to see things from another person's viewpoint. When people disagree with management, listen to their reasons. It may be that management is asking for too much commitment or too much change.

Admit when you are wrong. When another person's viewpoint is the correct approach, a good library manager is quick to admit that he or she is wrong. The old adage is true, "To err is human." Acknowledging that one is human and able to make mistakes encourages staff to make suggestions.

Use a sense of humor effectively. A good-natured chuckle is an excellent way to break tension. Often, a positive discussion begins with the catalyst of a clever quip or joke.

Be positive and gracious. People are more likely to grant requests if a library manger is friendly, sincere, positive, and approachable. A positive attitude indicates expectations of getting desired results. Psychologists say that one person's expectations can affect the behavior of another. A library manager who expects to get an affirmative reply and shows it in manner, speech, and body language is more likely to receive a "yes" than if he or she expects a negative response and displays self-fulfilling mannerisms.

Provide positive solutions. When members of the staff encounter problems, help them find positive solutions. Persuading people to try a solution is easier if it appears likely to solve their problem.

Let other people feel that the idea is theirs. Throughout this book on communications skills and effective leadership qualities is the theme that it is important to get a job accomplished, no matter who gets the credit. The successful manager encourages successful staff. Be generous. Think about the big picture. Don't be egotistical. Be a facilitator, not a dictator. Good leaders plant successful ideas and allow staff members to claim ownership as the ideas generate positive change and feedback.

Exercise strength of character, confidence, and respect. People respond more positively and meet more needs when they realize someone possesses strength of character, displays confidence, and commands respect.

The process of motivating staff includes meeting the needs of staff at the level of personal life, working conditions, status, and self-actualization. Managers recognize that most motivation of individuals comes from fellow members of a team.

REFERENCES

Blanchard, Kenneth, and Robert Lorber. 1984. *Putting the One-Minute Manager to Work*. New York: William Morrow.

Herzberg, Frederick, Bernard Mausner, and Barbara Block Snyderman. 1959. *The Motivation to Work*. 2d ed. New York: John Wiley.

Mazlow, Abraham. 1954. *Motivation and Personality*. New York: Harper & Row.

4

TEAM BUILDING

Library managers who build effective teams gain significant personal and career benefits. They find opportunities to draw talent, experience, and knowledge from a variety of people. They supervise people more effectively, and they work with staff for a common goal better than managers with weaker team-building skills. Team building encourages members of a group to examine how they work together and plan how to work more effectively. Effective managers have qualities and skills that build cohesiveness in a group, enabling the group to work together to achieve specific goals.

Library managers build teams for the "long haul" to offer efficient and effective services for library patrons. Teams require staff members to work as a unit. They support traditional library goals and objectives plus special projects and unusual events such as fund raisers and special programs that celebrate historic events. Team building gives library managers greater insight into individual differences and allows them to learn how to work with these differences and benefit from them. Team membership promotes a cooperative relationship as staff members work together to solve problems, and it improves communication pathways.

Traits of Effective Team Builders

Successful library managers who are effective team builders possess high self-esteem, positive attitudes, confidence, and open lines of communication. They are good team players, and they know when to delegate.

High self-esteem. Secure people don't feel threatened by others, and they work for a truly win-win situation. Library managers with a good self-image build strong bonds of mutual respect, trust, and confidence with their staff.

Positive attitude. Library managers with positive attitudes assume that solutions are possible for all situations, and they foster that same attitude in their staff. Successful managers provide an emotional environment that promotes success in problem solving and meets stated goals.

Confidence. When library managers demonstrate confidence in their ability to manage others and make decisions, they foster mutual respect. Mutual respect helps people work together efficiently to accomplish tasks and reach goals.

Open lines of communication. Effective team building and quality performance rely on high levels of communication. Chapter 7 covers this topic in greater detail.

Good team player. A manager displays team leadership behavior through cooperation, not competition. This supportive behavior stimulates staff to display the same behavior and preserves a sense of individual worth and importance.

Ability to delegate. Successful library managers know when to delegate. All managers with good team-building skills use delegation to direct, improve, and reward staff performance

Delegating Work

Delegating work and responsibilities is often one of the most difficult behaviors for a manager to learn, but it is essential for building effective teams. To delegate effectively, a library manager must give assignments, provide clear directions, gain a commitment from staff members to perform their jobs satisfactorily, grant staff appropriate authority to complete tasks, explain the timing and process for evaluations, and let staff do their own work with confidence.

Analyze the project. Analyze the project and set up standards for results and control. Prepare the necessary instructions for completing the project. When necessary, divide the project into units and distribute them to various staff members.

Know your staff. Know your staff members and their qualifications, expertise, and needs. Plan tasks assignments to use the best people for each job.

Assign tasks. Assign specific tasks to individuals, assign responsibility for completion, and provide clear instructions. Answer any questions concerning the project because good information about the entire project helps staff complete their individual parts.

Make staff responsible for their tasks. Delegation is synonymous with empowerment. When management gives staff responsibility for making decisions, staff understands that management trusts them. Encourage staff to discuss ways to modify the tasks if that will help finish the project on time. Allowing staff to offer and implement suggestions makes them an essential part of any team and gives them a sense of being in control.

Assess the results. Give staff an understanding of the criteria for assessment. They need to understand the evaluation process for themselves, their unit or part, and the final product.

Common Barriers to Delegation

Successful library managers overcome barriers to delegation. Often, employees need training to understand their jobs and take on delegated responsibilities. Although it takes time to teach employees new tasks, thorough training eventually saves time and produces effective staff members.

After installation of a new circulation system, one library circulation clerk consistently made errors. Materials on the shelf were incorrectly declared unavailable. Some patrons received invalid overdue notices, and the library lost books when other patrons failed to receive proper recalls for overdue materials. When Tom became responsible for this clerk, he quickly understood the need for more training. After the clerk received more training, errors became minimal.

There are many sources for problems when a manager delegates tasks. One major barrier is a lack of trust in an employee's preparation for accepting responsibility. Another is a prejudicial opinion about a staff member's inability to perform. Staff response to a particular management style may be a barrier. People perform differently under different management styles. The Omnipotence Syndrome, where managers think they are the only ones who can do the job well or faster than anyone else, is another obstacle to effective delegation. Lack of time to delegate is another problem. Ironically, some library managers say they cannot take time to delegate because they are too busy.

Some library managers are apprehensive about making staff members look good. Successful library managers refuse to let this barrier stand. They remain focused on what is important—not who does the work, but successful and timely completion of the task or project. Exceptional staff members are not a threat to a confident manager. After all, the measure of success for library managers and their programs is usually based on the performance of an entire staff. If a staff member has a talent, successful library managers proudly use that person to the fullest and consider themselves fortunate.

Basic Steps to Team Building

It is no small feat to meet a goal by managing a group of people who represent different backgrounds, experiences, skill levels, age groups, and personalities. Successful library managers build a team by focusing on a series of specific actions.

Focus on competencies when assigning team members. Analyze the skills of staff to identify those who are self-starters, those who enjoy what they do, and those who take pride in their work. Lawler makes the following suggestions concerning choosing team members.

- Select people with a working knowledge of the situation.

- Clearly articulate the expected outcomes and standards.

- Provide the resources and the authority to do the job. This means making available the necessary information, training, tools, money, and decision-making power.

- Set up a timetable for the planning and problem solving.

- Enable information to flow upward and downward.

- Periodically review progress with the groups.

- Tie rewards to performance and make sure the groups doing the work value the proffered rewards. (Lawler 1986)

To determine the best person for each task, library managers need to know the education, talents, skills, and previous team experience of the staff. Managers need to learn whether a staff member is task- or people-oriented, and they need to assess a person's willingness to undertake additional training if lacking necessary skills.

Establish clear team goals and clearly communicate desired results. Have definite objectives in mind and ensure that each member understands the team's goals and what the team needs to accomplish. Create an atmosphere of enthusiasm. Be sensitive to the needs of the group. Allow time for members to invest in the goals and make them their own.

Establish time limits and set deadlines and ground rules at the first meeting. Devoting attention to details in the beginning of a project often prevents power struggles, miscommunications, and responsibility avoidance. Clear rules and regulations allow a library manager to later make fair decisions about the project based on predetermined standards. Give the group guidelines for their work, and evaluate them without changing the rules.

Involve each member of the team in the project. Give each member an individual assignment or one as part of a small group. Use individual talents. Take advantage of opportunities for personal growth of staff members. Clearly define and communicate each assignment.

Maintain a results-oriented team structure. After members receive assignments and the project begins, make sure they clearly understand their assignments. Don't make assumptions or take anything for granted. A results-oriented library manager monitors team progress to assure everyone is on track. Frequent feedback reduces misunderstandings and builds positive experiences. Maintain open, honest, and timely communications between members and the leader. Team members need to acquire and practice skills such as conflict management, effective listening, and verbal and nonverbal communication; management positions do not have a monopoly on these skills. Exercise patience and cooperation in building a team.

Provide a collaborative climate, sharing power. Members who work well together are more likely to accomplish goals. When members feel free to ask for assistance from each other, library managers do not need to intervene as often. Leaders gain, not lose, power when teams share responsibility and authority. Group members work more effectively together, and they meet objectives and goals more efficiently and with less stress.

Strive for consensus. Collect opinions from all members, explore all sides of each issue, and get agreement from the group on solutions. Consensus brings stronger commitment from the team to the ultimate decision.

Implement the principles of motivation. To satisfy a vision, meet goals, and fulfill library objectives, a library manager needs strong skills of motivation. For more information on this topic, see chapter 3.

Build confidence. Make it possible for each member to feel important and essential. Team members should feel capable of successfully fulfilling their assignments. Confidence in job performance establishes self-esteem and independence of thought. It creates an atmosphere for more cooperative action in achieving team goals.

Build trust and respect. Team members must earn trust and mutual respect from each other, and the process often takes time. Good leaders set an example of these qualities, along with honesty and sincerity.

Be flexible. Team members and team leaders function better if all can adapt to change when necessary. If meeting a specific goal requires a new approach, everyone on the team needs to be flexible in making the change.

Furnish external support and recognition. Provide immediate recognition for individual and group accomplishments, and recognize them again when they meet major goals. Examples of recognition and rewards include extra time off; special social gatherings honoring the members; newspaper articles; television announcements stating names and accomplishments; public recognition in front of colleagues, family, or another supervisor; letters of recognition with copies sent to higher, influential authorities; plaques; gifts; or opportunities for greater responsibilities or larger projects.

Problems in Team Building and How to Solve Them

Calling a group a team, however, does not necessarily turn that group into a team. Library managers face challenges to leadership of the team, members' perceptions of equality, promotion of discipline, and level of performance.

Leaders of effective teams make decisions. They seek suggestions from their group, but they perform without calling for group votes on how to do the leader's job. There is usually one domineering personality in any group discussion, especially in a group that is working together as a team. Don't thwart anyone's enthusiasm, but do establish a format that limits discussion time for any one person. Redirect people who dominate discussions by asking them to put additional information or ideas in a memo for future consideration when more time is available.

If two people on your team have a problem working closely together, ask both to write down a description of their jobs as they see them every day. This activity is known as a polarization of ideas.

Compare the results to find some agreement, some gray areas, and some unaccomplished tasks that each person considers the other's job. Implement the technique further by asking both people to write down the activities they engage in every day in three categories: essential, important, and routine. Ask both people to meet and compare their perceptions. Point out misunderstandings, duplications of effort, ambiguities, and gaps in policies and procedures. This process gives each person a better understanding of the tasks and helps them coordinate the work and make better progress. Library managers know that everyone on a high-performing team is not equal. Some people have more responsibility than others. Some people get paid more or have more influence.

Unclear communication of goals is another obstacle in team building. Make sure to communicate instructions and desires clearly. Ask the team to provide feedback at intervals to ensure they understand assignments and make adequate progress on schedule.

Asking team members for a unified commitment to achieve the common goals helps avoid any hidden lack of initiatives from individuals. Present a positive attitude that they will meet the goals, and offer appropriate group achievement rewards.

Discussions that are not constructive often emerge during team meetings. Use good leadership skills to keep discussions germane to the subject, and remind members of their duties and objectives.

Team meetings are often boring. To energize meetings, successful library managers use innovative ideas, including new challenges and rewards. Request status of challenges already in place. Suggest a change in meeting place, time, or pace. Good teams have good discipline. People must arrive on time, fulfill responsibilities, and meet deadlines for achieving goals.

At one time or another, most teams fall into a creative slump. No one presents fresh ideas. A library manager is responsible for remedying creative slumps. Change the makeup of the team or give them more exciting assignments.

CRITERIA FOR ASSESSING THE SUCCESS OF TEAM PERFORMANCE

After establishing teams, library managers need to monitor the team's function and level of performance. Winning teams do not offer a haven for poor performers. They actually increase the pressure for individual performances.

Expect successful team members to

- participate in the plan.

- recognize how they best set goals, share in the work, and relate to each other.

- share data for the benefit of the team.

- discuss perceptions of issues, problems, and working relationships.

- analyze problems and contributing factors.

- plan specific actions to solve problems and concur with individuals assigned to implement them.

- share their evaluations of team performance.

All library managers must handle occasional mistakes. Give the team a chance to explain and work with them on a solution. Accept certain mistakes as inevitable. Convey the idea that everyone learns from mistakes and remind them that prudent risk-taking in pursuit of goals and objectives should continue even if it means making some mistakes.

REFERENCES

Lawler, E. E. 1986. *High-Involvement Management: Participative Strategies for Improving Organizational Performance.* San Francisco: Jossey-Bass.

5

PROBLEM SOLVING

Two important functions library managers perform are solving problems and making decisions. To do either effectively, it is important to understand how interpersonal relations affect the processes and to incorporate interpersonal skills into the process. Advance plans for approaching problem solving and decision making reduce anxieties of the process.

Problem-Solving Strategies

A good beginning for problem solving is to learn how to prevent a problem; therefore, the first strategy for problem solving is prevention. For example, before problems arise concerning travel expenses, bring staff members together and show them how to apply for permission to attend a conference and a workshop. Establish either a cap for housing and other per diem costs or an estimated cost for travel and housing. Then, make sure they understand if or when they need receipts for expenditures.

Avoid assigning blame when problems surface. Talk in terms of what is best for the common good, using the pronouns "our" and "we" in discussing the problem and solution. When small problems arise, people tend to blame or criticize, but that usually escalates the problem and prevents working to correct the mistakes.

Rather, bring the involved parties together and say, "We're beginning here and now to move forward on this task. From this point on, we will work to correct the situation." Use the same advice football coaches give their teams: "Always do your best. When you return to the locker room at the end of the game, leave it all on the field. Don't replay what you might have done or what someone else might have done. There is another game next week."

Mac is the district coordinator of a large school district. He determines that it is time to install a district-wide, online catalog system. He meets regularly with all the managers of the school library media centers, and they collaborate from the start in the planning process. Together, they visit districts with online systems, meet with vendors of systems, and attend workshops and conferences where systems are demonstrated. Mac and the managers meet often to discuss the project and brainstorm about goals and potential problems that their plan takes into consideration. All are proud of the subsequently successful installation of an online catalog system.

To minimize problems, library managers should also keep staff and patrons fully informed. Sharing timely, accurate information shows others that management cares about what they are doing and feels they are important to the organization. Good library managers cannot expect staff members to complete pieces of a puzzle if they don't know how the big picture looks. Good communication wards off gossip, inaccuracies, assumptions, and bigger problems.

Break down problems and take one step at a time to solve an issue or concern. It is overwhelming to try to accomplish everything at once, and it is difficult to rethink alternatives without an open mind for future steps and solutions.

Some problems are best left to solve themselves. For example, if a staff member cannot or will not carry out a designated assignment, that member's team may help solve the problem. The team may divide the assignment into several duties that get the job done and engages the problem staff member in some parts of the process.

PROBLEM-SOLVING STEPS

Consider the following steps when solving problems.

Identify the problem. Find out the "where" and "what" of the problem. Identify the manifestations. Find out if the problem lies within one individual or between individuals, within a group or between groups, or within a system.

Find out why the problem exists and if there are any unmet needs. Look at the situation from the point of view of all the people involved. Consider the *real* (what is actually happening) and the *ideal* (what the manager would like to have happen). Determine if the *ideal* is achievable in the immediate future or if a short-term solution is logical. If staff performance is a major part of the problem, consider the following questions.

- What leadership, decision-making, and problem-solving skills does the library manager have? How do they match the needs of the staff members? Does the manager meet staff expectations?

- What commitment does the library manager have to the objectives or motivation of others?

- What are the needs of the people involved? What training do staff members need? Do staff members feel secure or need to increase their self-esteem? Do they need an opportunity to grow professionally or personally? Do they feel a sense of belonging to a group? (For further discussion of personal needs, see chapter 4.)

A good library manager uses these questions to understand his or her relationship to problems. If uncertain about the problem, ask staff for help.

Analyze the problem or concern. An outgrowth of problem identification is determining why the problem exists. Suggest that people write a few sentences describing the situation: who, what, how, and when. They must focus on current issues rather than past events, conflicts, or anger that may have little bearing on the current situation. Confront the issue, not the person. Describe feelings and views objectively while defining the problem and analyzing how it developed.

It is important that those involved agree on a description of the problem or concern. Although some people assume this is a simple matter, it is a significant phase in the process of problem solving and decision making. Superficial attention to this leads later to backtracking or basing conclusions on inaccuracies or irrelevancies. Defining the problem allows for differing perceptions and opinions and results in a broadening of perspectives. To achieve the maximum understanding of a problem situation, library managers must solicit diverse ideas and opinions.

Effective library managers recognize common behavioral barriers to problem identification. For example, some people feel it is easier to work around a problem than to face it squarely. As discussed in chapter 2, this sets up a lose-win situation that is potentially destructive for the group. Some people do not want to admit that there is a problem, so they ignore it. Those who have the most to win or lose are often the least objective in evaluating the situation. Part of analyzing problems and concerns is considering objectives. What objectives will meet the established goal? Project a resolution of the problem and decide how to describe the original problem for someone. Speculate on desired results and accomplished objectives. If someone resolves the situation, how will people behave?

Search for a solution. After defining and analyzing the problem, clarify the objective and begin to generate alternative solutions. Have staff members list possible outcomes and generate alternative methods to meet the objectives. Brainstorming creates more ideas and finds better solutions.

Encourage risk-taking. Discuss how team members can help each other reach their own goals and the stated common goal. Evaluate the alternatives and list the advantages and disadvantages to the solution, including feelings and facts. List things that affect individuals and the group. Consider time and resources available. Include risks and drawbacks or negative factors.

Make a decision. A successful library manager guides those involved in the problem or concern in selecting the most feasible solution. In decision making, show how each person can profit. Effective decisions

- solve the problem rather than meet immediate needs

- provide methods that are easy to apply

- fit within the staff, budget, collection, and facility constraints.

Reach a consensus. Reaching a consensus means coming to an agreement or decision as a group. It includes a free and open exchange of ideas until reaching the agreement. It hears and understands each person's concerns and ideas and makes a sincere attempt to work for a solution that either benefits all or meets the stated objectives. In consensus decision making, participants try to foresee any possible consequences of the agreed-upon solution. Unforeseen circumstances can destroy seemingly good solutions.

Sue is a media specialist at a high school. She emerges elated from a school board meeting where the superintendent presented and the board accepted the district's five-year technology plan.

Two months ago, Sue accepted a challenge to head a technology committee for the district and develop a plan to present to the school superintendent. She began by sending humorous memos to all faculty asking for their participation on a technology committee. She offered incentives of continuing education credits and a voice in allocation of the dollars.

Teachers in each school chose a representative who met with all their departmental or grade-level colleagues and devised their school's plan. From there, the district group met and discussed the general needs of the school district and made a list of each school's unique needs. At each meeting, they discussed types of equipment and matched quality to quantity to get the best technology for most applications. During the final meetings, each school representative presented their minimum requests.

By working closely as a team and spending significant meeting time in listening, the group reached a unanimous agreement on the final plan. The consensus agreement from all schools in the district facilitated approval of the plan when presented to the superintendent, and his favorable support helped gain approval from the school board.

Implement the decision. Translate the jointly designed solution into a plan of action. Agree on how and when to carry out the plan. Implementing the decision may mean implementing change. Changes in knowledge are usually easier to make than changes in attitude or individual behavior. Staff accepts technical information about new technologies more easily than it accepts any changes required in personal habits or duties.

Changing individual behavior requires the establishment of short-range goals with achievement limits of less than one year. Communicate goals to all affected people and outline how the decision was made, how it will benefit the staff members, and what new responsibilities result.

Evaluate the solution. Review action plans after implementing activities. If the solution is resolving the problem, continue the activities. If not, repeat the process from the beginning to choose an alternative solution.

Using People Skills to Help Solve Problems

Effective library managers use people skills to create a favorable environment that makes problem solving and decision making more successful. Use the following tips to make the decision-making process work more smoothly.

- Say "we" rather than "I." No library manager can accomplish tasks alone, and it helps to let staff members know they will share in the credit. "When you use 'we,' you also share the credit. It doesn't cost you a thing to acknowledge another person's contribution" (Kouzes and Posner 1988, 153).

- Create a climate that allows for interaction. Provide spaces and opportunities for individuals to work together on the problem.

- If consensus is not possible, put questions to a vote.

- Avoid spending excessive time on minor problems. Make a reasonable decision and move on to the next task.

- Use time as a resource and work through the process to get the best solution. For example, meet in small groups and ask for alternative solutions. Take time to find out if there is a diversity of opinion; if so, find out why.

- Choose an environment that is conducive to the task and has limited distractions.

- Encourage everyone to participate.

- Listen actively.

- Check the perceptions of the group.

- Separate fact from opinion.

- Separate personalities from issues.

- Minimize the need for the group to form coalitions.

- Help the group understand and acknowledge that one solution may not please everyone.

- If a bad decision is made, suggest a quick way to change the situation or give the problem to team members and let them brainstorm solutions.

There is always some resistance to the process of problem solving, and library managers need to maintain control. Consider the following behaviors that help a manager overcome resistance and keep control of the problem-solving process.

- Be a positive person. Think and act positively.

- Be empathetic when someone is resisting emotionally.

- Keep focused on what the person needs to know.

- Do not become distracted from the issue.

- Use a successful example when attempting to focus on a different direction.

- Be supportive of other opinions, acknowledging their validity.

- Introduce new information that supports or presents a new direction.

Group Problem Solving

Library managers who are effective leaders help groups solve problems and concerns. They set the stage, keep the discussion moving, develop wide participation, and help groups establish a systematic approach to each task. Sometimes, a library manager's biggest challenge is retaining leadership in a group problem-solving situation.

First, define the problem. Focus the group's attention on its basic task and purpose. It is important to phrase the topic of discussion clearly in language the entire group understands. A well-stated question stimulates constructive and creative participation.

Next, ask the group for a broadly defined solution. Work toward a more narrowly defined, shared decision. Test for group consensus by occasionally reviewing points developed during the discussion. Avoid the temptation to give answers. During group problem-solving sessions, it is not the manager's function to lecture or instruct. The group is responsible for finding the answers. Occasionally identify and summarize the group's conclusions, however, because they may not recognize their own success.

Finally, ask for alternate solutions. To stimulate discussion, offer suggestions by using an "if" statement. Get members of the group to cite reasons for their support of the various answers to the problem. Solicit options on which solution offers the most promise for progress. Try to achieve a consensus (unanimous) decision from the group.

Hints for Group Problem Solving

All library managers face the challenge of encouraging group participation.

- Recognize when an individual wants to say something and provide that person with an adequate opportunity to contribute. Call the group's attention to unheard contributions, prompting reticent people who possess important information.

- Help the group understand the meaning and intent of individual contributions.

- Maintain the continuity of discussion by pointing out any similarities among ideas offered by different members.

- Encourage group discussion rather than member–leader discourse.

- Convey acceptance of group decisions by exhibiting a noncritical attitude and refraining from evaluating individual contributions. Remain impartial in spite of having strong opinions on any discussion. The same principle applies here as governs the conduct of the chairperson under parliamentary rules or the moderator of a panel discussion: The prestige of leadership gives the leader's view more weight than that of others, thus the leader must not use that position unfairly by expressing personal views. Also, once a manager becomes involved as a protagonist, expressing and defending personal views, there is no time to perform the real functions of leadership.

- Bring in those who are not talking by making them feel that the group welcomes their contributions.

- Call on people by name only if they are likely to make a worthwhile contribution. Do not unnecessarily embarrass reluctant members.

- Do not monopolize the meeting. In most groups, participants bring special knowledge and skills. As a manager, know what assets each person possesses and make sure they are available to the group. Still, prevent any one person—the leader, a plaintiff, an expert, etc.—from dominating the discussion.

- Keep the discussion moving and on the subject. Keeping discussions moving at a brisk pace is desirable, but do not move it faster than the group wants to go. Patience is an important attribute of a good library manager as leader. Some diversions are fruitful, but only allow them when they relate to the main topic.

- Help the group bring out logical fallacies and errors in reasoning, but don't push too hard or too fast along these lines. Don't fit the discussion rigidly into a preconceived pattern nor use cross-examination when the result makes people look foolish.

Obstacles to Group Problem Solving

There are many pitfalls in the process of problem solving.

- Don't say that the group should move slowly. This allows the group to avoid getting started and inhibits them setting their own pace for attacking the problem.

- Don't find a scapegoat and "ride" that person. This focuses the group's energy on evaluating and defending members rather than attending to the task at hand.

- Don't set up another proposal in opposition every time someone brings up another proposal and then conclude that a middle ground represents the best course of action. This assures indecisiveness or no action at all.

- Don't say that the problem is irrevocably tied to other problems. This tells the group they cannot solve the problem until they solve all the other problems. This precluded any action.

- Don't say that the problem is one that occurs everywhere. This is a rationalization for its existence, not a solution.

- Don't retreat into general objectives agreeable to everyone without suggesting content changes. This reinforces the status quo.

- Don't appoint a committee; table the problem until a future date; notice that time is up and everyone is very busy; or conclude that participants clarified their thinking on the problem and how beneficial that is. These are all delaying tactics, not solution tactics.

- Don't look slightly embarrassed when someone brings up the real problem. Don't hint that it is in bad taste to articulate it; that it is too premature to discuss; that it is subject to misrepresentation, or that it might suffer from misinterpretation by outsiders.

Running a library effectively is a difficult job, and one of the most important functions for a library manager is problem solving and implementing change. The library staff members need to work well together as a team, and a successful library manager practices good people skills and encourages staff to participate in problem solving and decision making.

References

Kouzes, James M., and Barry Z. Posner. 1988. *The Leadership Challenge: How to Get Extraordinary Things Done in Organizations.* San Francisco: Jossey-Bass.

6

CONFLICT MANAGEMENT

In any group, conflict is inevitable. The workplace has characteristics that build interdependent relationships among diverse people with different viewpoints. In a work group or organization, people see the needs of the organization differently because of their various job orientations. Staff members working together for a common goal may generate conflict when people have different ideas on who should do each task and in what way. To achieve a win-win solution, all members must apply conflict management skills.

Principles of Conflict

In *Leadership Skills: Standout Performance for Human Resources Managers*, William Tracey provides a valuable list of basic principles that define conflict situations (Tracey 1990, 157-158).

It is inevitable. Conflict will happen because of human nature. Working together in close proximity over time will cause disagreements because of the personalities of those in the workplace and their diverse reactions to situations. People with problems in their personal lives may unconsciously bring their attitudes to work.

It is predictable. To the extent that certain situations exist between different types of individuals, it is possible to predict conflict. For example, aggressive staff members who are vying for promotions cause conflict in their efforts to move to the next rung on the ladder.

It is proportional to the organization. The larger the organization, the more employees will interact with each other with more chances for disagreement. A two-person library with a director and a clerk has less opportunity for conflict to occur. In larger organizations, disagreement between ways to accomplish tasks may occur in a direct proportion to the numbers who are working on the assignment.

It can be disastrous if excessive. Patrons and administrators quickly notice warring staff members. Staff conduct may "spill over" into their relationships with professionals outside the department and the library users' environment. If people take sides in such disagreements, it weakens everyone's efforts as sabotage begins and the situation disintegrates.

It is preventable. Library managers can lessen the stress and tension that cause or worsen many conflicts. Watch for signs that the staff needs recognition or assistance. Notice when staff encounters problems at home and in the workplace. Look for causes of friction within departments. When staff wants change that management cannot accommodate, explain why such change is not possible in the immediate future. Staff members are less likely to aggravate a conflict when they know that management acknowledges the problem and agrees to seek a solution.

It is complex. It is often difficult for a library manager to unearth the real cause of a conflict. A staff member may cite one reason for a conflict when, in reality, something totally different is at the base of the problem. Discovering the cause of conflict is more difficult than determining a patron's real reason for asking a reference question. Nevertheless, library managers need some of the same interpersonal skills to resolve both mysteries.

It is risky. It is difficult to separate two people in a fight, whether it is a physical, mental, or emotional conflict. Policemen and bystanders who try to separate fighters often find themselves the "punching bag" when the fighters turn their anger on the person interfering. The less information a library manager holds, the more difficult settling disputes becomes. Understanding all sides of a misunderstanding includes the history of all staff members involved in the dispute. With this information, a library manager begins to determine solutions *before* meeting with the group.

It is symptomatic. If a new conflict flares up immediately after another one settles, library managers need to determine root causes for conflict in their organization. They need to review the reporting structure for library staffing, the status of job assignments, the strength of expectations for rewards, and the individual personalities of people who are working together. Identify disagreements before a conflict escalates.

Sources of Conflict

Conflict originates for a variety of reasons:

An atmosphere of caring exists. Productive conflict arises when people care about one another. When people care enough about each other and shared goals, they accept the emotional risks of raising and discussing controversial issues as they try to improve the situation.

Unexplained or misunderstood change. Moving new technologies into departments with little or no prior discussion, training, or warning generates destructive conflict from staff members. Anger that management does not appear to understand these expanded job performance expectations causes stress, and stress results in conflict.

Different needs, values, and perceptions are present. Differing needs, values, and perceptions produce conflict. People will often misunderstand and misjudge people when they have incomplete or distorted information. Bring misunderstandings into the open; otherwise, it is virtually impossible for people to move ahead as a team.

Interdependency is a factor. The actions of one person create consequences for other people. This sometimes leads to conflict. Open communication about the reasons for certain actions or changes, and open discussion of the consequences of these actions will reduce the conflict caused by interdependency.

Mike and Millie, two reference librarians in a public library, worked in partitioned areas. The library manager moved Millie to a larger space with more comfortable chairs and a scenic view. Mike continued to handle telephone reference questions from his cubicle.

When Millie and Mike became argumentative, the library manager called both into her office. Mike felt slighted, Millie felt rewarded, and neither one apparently understood the true reason for the change. The library manager explained that Millie preferred to work with patrons in person, and Mike preferred answering patron's questions over the telephone. She adjusted the working spaces to give each person the proper environment to do their job effectively.

Concern about limited resources. When there are not enough materials or personnel to get the job done, competition for the scarce resources causes conflict.

Unequal rewards and praise. When people feel one person or group received more rewards or praise than another, resentment arises. If the organization dispenses rewards based only on an individual's work, it reinforces competition instead of cooperation.

Goals and deadlines differ. Concern about meeting different goals generates conflict. When different people have different deadlines, they don't assume mutual cooperation. They expect the "other group" is ignoring or blocking their earnest efforts. Conflict also occurs when personal values clash with those of the library program. For example, offering materials on all sides of an issue to patrons to meet the Library Bill of Rights may cause conflict with staff members if some of the material is against the teachings of their religion.

Fear of losing power, position, job, or control. Fears of this nature prevail in many organizations and professions. These fears are greater when poor economic conditions exist or when there is intense competition among people. Changing organizational charts, job descriptions, location of an office, or the numbers or types of jobs assigned to different employees generates fear of lost power and causes conflict because there are gains and losses in change.

Beneficial Conflict

Not all conflict is bad, however. How library managers handle conflict makes the difference between productive and destructive outcomes. A supervisor's attitude toward conflict resolution determines whether conflict is beneficial for an organization or group. According to Tracey (1990, 158), beneficial conflict may

- reveal and clarify important issues

- offer opportunities for managers to learn more about themselves and their attitudes and behavior, explore the perceptions of others, and develop more productive and satisfying work relationships

- help managers identify underlying problems, ameliorate or eliminate negative attitudes and feelings, correct misunderstandings, and generate the commitment needed for change

- serve as a relief valve for dissatisfaction or strong negative feelings

- actuate major changes, innovation, and creativity in finding solutions to problems

KNOWLEDGE, ATTITUDES, AND SKILLS IN MANAGING CONFLICT

Managing conflict is a mixture of knowing oneself and understanding others. Knowing personal strengths, weaknesses, skills, and limitations helps a library manager predict reactions in confrontational situations. Few people have an accurate assessment of their ability to handle confrontational situations. Library managers benefit from attending workshops to analyze strengths and limitations in conflict management and formulate plans to expand skills. Courses of study and workshop experiences in conflict management help a library manager recognize his or her probable reaction to stressful situations and improve these skills.

Possess a thorough knowledge of others. Learn about staff members' needs, wants, biases, and motivations by talking with them in relaxed situations. When a library manager understands that a staff member was up most of the night with a sick child, it is easier to understand confrontational behavior. By understanding others, the manager can act in ways that preserve dignity and self-respect.

Avoid defensiveness. Instead of being defensive, fearful, or angry, focus on the other person. Leave the problem where it belongs, with the person who has the problem. Learn how to diffuse anger and frustration. Books on assertiveness training will offer help on developing some strategies to cope with such stressful situations. Defensive or aggressive behavior puts others on the defensive.

Improve your problem-solving skills. An effective library manager always tries to see both sides of a dispute, even when there is a personal or management bias for one position. In the case of a dispute between two staff members, treat each side fairly. Be receptive while maintaining an objective vision of the situation.

Use your problem-solving skills. Apply problem-solving skills using observation and inquiry to identify and analyze a problem and seek a solution. Use paraphrasing. Restate to clarify the statement or problem. (For example, "Are you saying . . . ." or "If I understood you correctly . . . .") Concentrate on the facts or issues.

Engage in active listening. Pay attention to the words of the speaker and watch body language. When replying, paraphrase or clarify all other positions in the discussion. As a listener, restate relevant facts. It is important to let others know they are heard, understood, and accepted. Encourage others to talk freely without interruptions. Listen for hidden meanings. A library manager needs to use all available communication and persuasion skills.

Diagnosing Conflict

When trying to diagnose a conflict, decide whether the conflict is an ideological or value conflict, a "real" or tangible conflict, or a combination of both. Value conflicts are exceedingly difficult to negotiate. If, for example, it is very difficult to establish a mutually acceptable position for two people when one believes in the privilege of displaying political messages on their clothing while another rejects the appropriateness of staff endorsing political issues in the library. If it is a conflict of values resulting in no tangible effects on either party, consider tolerating it. If, however, a tangible effect exists, resolve that element of the conflict. The impact on library funding is hard to predict if library employees use the library to promote a political party. Who wins and who loses? Is the winner grateful? Is the loser bitter? Does the library win or lose? Discuss value conflicts with staff so that they understand the policy even if some don't agree.

Resolving Conflict

Many approaches exist for resolving conflicts, but no method applies to all situations or to all personalities. A library manager must decide on the best approach, when to employ it, and with whom it will work. When a method works successfully, there is a tendency to overuse it. Learning about other means of handling conflict gives library managers a wider choice of actions to employ and makes them better able to tailor the response.

As a rule, cooperation among staff members is the best method for managing conflict. It offers the best solution, a win-win solution. Combined with collaboration and integration, cooperation requires that all people involved in the conflict recognize the abilities and expertise of others. The group acknowledges each individual's position, but they place an emphasis on trying to solve the problem, not defend a particular position or faction. Everyone fully expects to modify the original views as work progresses, and they see conflict as a natural process that leads to helpful, creative solutions. When emotions are at their highest during the conflict, this model allows people to work through their emotions. Ultimately, a cooperative solution emerges that lets both sides feel victorious.

Jane, the library media specialist, modified policy and eliminated the restrictions on the number of resources individual students could check out because budget increases during the past year provided for additional resource acquisitions.

Henry, a circulation aide with a very controlling personality, thought the change would increase his work load of handling overdue books and would create a scarcity of available resources in a specific area. Instead of talking to Jane, Henry complained to other staff members and sought support for his point of view.

When someone informed her of the problem, Jane called a staff meeting to identify the pros and cons of both policies and air staff concerns. They reached a consensus to use the new policy for a trial period of six weeks. If it caused no problems, it would stand. The trial period did not create much difference in the work load or availability of resources. Henry accepted the new policy, and the entire staff relaxed.

Negotiation is another means of resolving conflict. When using negotiating skills, keep people and issues separate so that staff does not react negatively to a solution that is too closely tied to a particular person. Give information freely so staff can make the best choice.

A good negotiator controls discussion and allows each person to state an opinion and a solution while keeping any one person from monopolizing the discussion. Control the discussion and ask speakers to keep strategies positive.

Although the terms *avoidance, denial,* and *suppression* often carry negative connotations, library managers may successfully use such approaches to resolve a conflict.

Avoidance is a conflict management method used when issues are not important. It allows for a cooling-off period and time for further considerations. People sometimes use this method to sidestep issues or avoid responsibility for making decisions. To counteract avoidance, set a deadline, seek out and define reasons for resistance and inactivity, or make decisions easy by eliminating distractions.

When the issue or the timing is not critical, denial may be the most productive way of dealing with conflict, but an effective library manager monitors the conflict to ensure it does not escalate.

People who play down differences use suppression. Employ suppression when it is more important to preserve a relationship than to deal with an insignificant issue through conflict.

Power is another approach to settling differences. Authority or position is often the source of power, but it may take the form of a majority or a persuasive minority. Sometimes, where other forms of handling conflict are clearly inappropriate, using power is effective. Using power to resolve conflicts is appropriate if there is a lack of knowledge or expertise; if the situation requires quick, decisive action; or if someone must implement unpopular decisions. Use this strategy sparingly.

When library managers need to foster feelings of harmony and goodwill, accommodation may be the best approach to conflict resolution. Accommodation elevates another person and makes them feel better about an issue. Accommodation also plays down differences among people while looking for a common ground. This method offers a library manager an opportunity to give way to a better position if there is uncertainly of position or suspicion of a mistake. By accommodating people, a library manager buys time to assess situations and survey alternatives. Accommodating is a useful tool when a library manager works with someone who has a great deal of power.

Conflicts frequently end through compromise. Although often used to settle differences (and often regarded as a virtue in our culture), the compromise approach risks serious setbacks. Sometimes, however, compromise makes sense, as when there are insufficient resources to accomplish a win-win solution, and a manager wants to forestall a win-lose situation. In a trade-off situation, the opponent has equal power, and everyone is committed to mutually exclusive goals. Compromise also achieves temporary settlements to complex issues.

Library managers need to know different methods of dealing with conflict. People become more effective in handling conflict once they know the methods and their advantages, but counterproductive elements always hover in the background.

- Don't let conflict become the agenda. Take care of it immediately and go on to other issues.

- Avoid power struggles. Empower others. Allow others to take control of their feelings.

- Show real concern for both the problem and the people involved. Concern is an important ingredient in solving conflicts.

- Beware of overconfidence in perceiving motivations for actions of others. Library managers must not project their own beliefs as the standard, and they must not assume the same standards are shared by everyone

- Don't do all the talking. Do more listening.

- Don't be dogmatic or argumentative.

- Avoid exaggerating the problem. When anger enters the picture, exaggeration follows. Conflict is common in most organizations and groups, no matter how large or small. For more in-depth information on this subject, use sources in the bibliography. Additional information in the chapters on team building or problem solving and decision making in this book may also be helpful.

Giving Yourself the Advantage in Confrontation

Confrontation is a powerful experience. It can be either good or bad for the people involved. Confrontation often carries many negative connotations, but in itself it is not always negative. It may be positive when directed toward another person's strength or used as an encouragement to take action. The primary purpose of helpful confrontation should be to bring the conflicting individuals into a more direct understanding of the situation. Try to create an atmosphere where the individual explores and changes the behavior that hindered growth and development.

Handling Personal Confrontation

When handling personal confrontation, listen carefully to what the person is *not* saying. Watch for body language, incorporate the person's own words into a statement of the desired position. Reinforce the point of agreement, not disagreement. Share feelings and try to find common ground for conversation or a shared interest. Summarize the problem and invite a solution.

The circulation aide in the elementary school greeted Jack with a smile, but he angrily blamed the aide for mentioning an overdue book. With a pleasant voice, the aide reiterated Jack's concern and mellowed his anger. After a short discussion, Jack understood that other children needed a chance to read the lost book, and he agreed to look at home for it.

The following day, Jack's mother called the aide to say the book was not at home and must surely be in the school library. After verifying that the book was not in the library, the aide called Jack to her office and suggested they go together and search his locker. They found the book buried under some clothes belonging to his locker partner. The aide called Jack's mother and said they found the book.

Handling Surprise Confrontation

Often a confrontation happens when least expected. Don't be put unexpectedly on the defensive by an adversary. If a confrontation begins on the telephone, delay the conversation by arranging a time and place to meet. For example, if an irate patron calls, listen carefully and then suggest investigating the issue and calling them back within 24 hours.

A Six-Step Plan for Confrontation

If library managers do their homework and investigate the issues, they empower themselves to confront problems. An optimistic attitude and a belief in self are vital. Try the following six ways to deal with confrontation.

1. Look for openings and observe the behavior of adversaries.

2. Be clear on desired goals.

3. Determine whether personal environment factors can give an advantage.

4. Have a plan and follow it. Do homework early. Carry out the elements of each plan.

5. When the meeting is over, evaluate the successes and failures.

6. Review progress and plan ahead for the next time. If necessary, make changes.

Maintaining Control in Conflict Management

Maintaining control is a must in handling confrontation. Plan rebuttals for your opponent's oppositions. Decide what needs accomplished. Visualize under what conditions the encounter will take place. Try to have the confrontation take place in the library manager's office, thereby putting the conflict in the home court. This gives the manager an advantage over a less familiar setting.

Plan the meeting, and meet according to the plan. Know the desired outcome and what steps are necessary to make it happen. Use a comfortable method of contact and control the turf. Beware of intimidation or pressure by others.

Know the adversary's personality. Little is accomplished when someone loses control. Take care not to generate anger. When an adversary responds to specific types of information, research the problem and know the statistics, the relevant issues, the names of people who would be helpful, and other similar facts available for discussion.

Plan an image. Fair or not, people make judgments about others based on the way they look. Plan first impressions. Library managers may know themselves, but they have to win over other people. A library manager has to decide whether to "fit in" or be in direct conflict. Blending in with others gives a sense of belonging. In some situations, a library manager can improve the chances of winning by dressing more like the adversary. Enter a room with confidence, head high and chin high. Don't rush in like a charging bull. If a handshake is appropriate, do it briefly and firmly with confidence. Make the greeting brief, clear, relaxed, and confident. Use good posture because it adds confidence and conveys this feeling to others. If possible, choose a physical position that is slightly elevated over an adversary, but be careful not to make others feel defensive. Choose a position that allows good eye contact. Be well informed and prepared.

Plan communications. Use proper grammar and good diction to express control and confidence. Be careful of jargon. Be as natural and professional as possible. Do not bluff any expertise. If appropriate, use names of people who are important to an adversary, but do not overdo the name dropping. To support views, use citations from others such as, "According to . . ." This provides an alliance, even though that person may not be physically present.

When the meeting concludes, summarize the agreement. Get all adversaries to agree with the statement or volunteer to summarize the discussion in writing. Controlling the summarization allows a library manager to select the words and phrasing of conditions, agreements, and recommendations. Try to produce a win-win situation from the meeting.

Terminating an Employee

Most managers agree that termination is a last resort to solving a problem. Firing an employee is always a difficult decision. Before confronting an employee, make every effort to develop, counsel, and coach the person to meet established standards of performance. Unfortunately, some employees may not achieve or maintain acceptable performance in spite of proffered help.

Observe the following when considering termination of an employee.

- Make sure you are familiar with the legal ramifications of the termination of an employee. Not following proper procedures can result in a costly lawsuit for the organization and perhaps for the manager personally.

- Be sure firing is warranted. Increase supervision and feedback to the employee using good coaching techniques to encourage improvement. Be specific about problem areas.

- Involve the employee's supervisor in any interviews and in the evaluation of the performance after any coaching sessions or observation of the employee's performance.

- Document the employee's performance and interviews in writing. Make sure to date and sign the documentation, including signatures from the employee and any other of the employee's supervisors.

- Alert the employee to the possibility of termination and follow through on any other necessary formalities or policies required before termination occurs.

- Notify the employee of the schedule for a final interview.

- Tell the employee the cause for termination. If a referral to an internal or external group or person is appropriate, do this at the appropriate time.

Address conflict and poor performance as soon as they occur even though handling them may be the least pleasant assignment for any library manager. Additional pay for management positions takes this duty into account, and most library managers still feel they aren't paid enough to handle some conflict situations. However, not all conflict is bad. The clever library manager channels conflict into useful areas and improves all aspects of the library through well-managed conflict resolution.

References

Tracey, William R. 1990. *Leadership Skills: Standout Performance for Human Resources Managers*. New York: AMACOM.

7

COMMUNICATION SKILLS

Successful library managers know the power of good communication skills. They need skills for sending messages effectively because the way they send a message is as important as the message itself in everyday interaction with others.

Steve worked at the public library. On his drive to work one morning, he got a brilliant idea. A rearrangement of some seating space in the library would correct several noise problems. That morning, Steve approached his supervisor, Jeanne, in the hall with his suggestion. A week later, he asked Jeanne what she thought about his idea of moving the furniture to reduce the noise level in the reference section. She looked quizzical and asked, "What furniture? What move are you talking about?" Steve tried unsuccessfully to refresh her memory.

Discouraged but not defeated, Steve went back to his desk, and decided to take a more formal approach by submitting the proposal in writing. He stated the proposed idea. He drew a sketch. He used bullets to highlight the possible benefits, and he submitted the proposal to Jeanne that afternoon. The next morning, Jeanne met with Steve and reviewed the plans. She thanked him for presenting the idea in a clear and visual way and approved the plan.

Steve gave the situation some additional thought and realized he was by nature a face-to-face communicator while Jeanne was a very concrete, sequential thinker. Steve realized that in the future he needed to consider the other person's best learning and communication style for optimum results.

An effective communicator is aware of how assumptions and feelings affect how people understand another person's meaning. It is important to know how a manager affects an audience before building verbal bridges among staff members or making presentations to a wider audience. Communication skills include oral, nonverbal, social, written, and listening skills. This chapter includes proxemics, "the study of the ways humans use and communicate with space" (Richmond et al. 1991, 118).

Oral Communication Skills

The communication skill used most is oral. Most library managers prefer oral communication because it's handy, thorough, and complete. It's a good way to get viewpoints from others, and it fosters openness and accountability. Oral communication offers an opportunity to judge the other person's reactions quickly, respond to a listener's questions, and get immediate feedback. Some people are better auditory communicators than visual communicators; they need to hear rather than read information.

Library managers know that a person's attitude sends a message. A sentence given with a frown will affect the listener differently than the same sentence said with a smile. Any message presented with obvious enthusiasm is more likely to generate enthusiasm than one delivered in monotones from an expressionless face.

Language that is direct, simple, and familiar is the most powerful. In an age of information overload, some messages may not get through if given only once. Repeat the message and ask for a restatement if it is an important one.

Most people need to reflect on their ability to communicate orally.

- Decide in advance the outcome or purpose of the communication or conversation.

- Organize any thoughts about the situation.

- Ask for clarification if the message is not clear.

- Take action to improve performance.

- Avoid expressions like "uh," "ah," and "you know." Try tape-recording the messages and replay them at a later time.

- If there is bad news to communicate, do it quickly.

- When communicating information, make sure the receiver can use or benefit from the information.

- Be aware of others' emotions.

- Be direct—mean what you say and say what you mean. An open, honest communicator brings out the same in others.

- Don't be afraid to say, "I don't know." This provides an open and trusting environment.

- Use face-to-face communication whenever possible. Memos are often misunderstood.

- Learn to watch how people receive and decode the messages.

- Be careful of incongruity in communications. It can chip away at credibility.

- If communicating criticism, consider whether it is specific and comes out of goodwill. Depersonalize it when possible. A library manager can then choose to ignore it, agree with it, apologize if necessary, or deflect it.

- Keep in mind the receiver of any message. If there is a personality conflict, it is necessary to improve the relationship before effective communication can take place. Distrust, fear, and prejudice hamper and distort effective communication.

- Be sure to check that the receiver understands each message. People from various backgrounds may not interpret the same information in the same way.

- Avoid using jargon or technical language unless the receiver understands this language. If necessary, explain the meaning of the special language used.

Nonverbal Communication Skills

Nonverbal communication skills are also required in oral communications. Along with conveying a message, oral communication allows the recipient to observe the demeanor of the sender. Virginia Richmond tells us

> Throughout the almost 5,000 years of recorded history relating to the study of human communication, the primary focus of research and teaching about communication has centered on verbal messages. Not until the eighteenth century did communication scholars begin to pay serious attention to the role of nonverbal behavior in the communication process. (Richmond et al. 1991, 3)

This research suggests the importance of understanding nonverbal cues, such as gestures, eye contact, or appearance. These cues affect how people convey messages. A large percentage of the communication between people is nonverbal, and because it is unconscious, these cues can be a barrier or an aid to effect communication.

The effective library manager learns how to observe another person's nonverbal cues. Lin Gensing gives the following advice for reading another person's body language.

> It is hard to interpret the body language of a person with whom you are not well acquainted. If you want to be able to read people's nonverbal cues, become aware of their characteristic mannerisms.
>
> It is necessary to be aware of the context for someone's behavior.
>
> If possible, to avoid misunderstandings, confirm your interpretation of another person's behavior with that person. (Gensing 1991, 56)

Further, Richmond and others list the categories of nonverbal messages as physical appearance, gesture and movement, face and eye behavior, vocal behavior, space, touch, environment, scent and smell, and time (Richmond et al. 1991, 13-15).

- Gestures may aid the communication process by providing emphasis. Use them with discrimination, however, because over-gesturing can be distracting. Use hands naturally and realize that unconscious gestures may hinder communications.

Avoid distracting gestures, such as primping or tapping fingers that rob a person of credibility.

- Use facial expressions that are appropriate for the message sent.

- Eye contact is important in enhancing communication. People associate direct eye contact with competent, socially skilled, assertive and friendly individuals. To begin a conversation and get the attention of the other person, make eye contact. Look at the other person's face a majority of the time to show interest. Limit the length and frequency of glances in a conversation to establish authority.

- Posture creates an impression and influences communications. To enhance communication and listening skills, remember that leaning forward is an attentive posture. To promote free and open communications, adopt an attentive posture and combine this with signs of agreement, unfolded arms, and uncrossed knees. Try to sit at the same level as the other person.

- When looking at written material, look at the material with the other person. Point out important items.

- Shake hands as appropriate. Be the first to extend a hand. Use a firm, brief grip.

- People send nonverbal messages by the way they dress. For better or worse, people often make assumptions about others' personalities and characters based on appearance. Wear clothing that is appropriate for the environment or situation. Observe how others dress. People often like and align themselves with someone who dresses like them because they anticipate more understanding in the conformity.

In developing social skills, notice how body language affects communications and adjust appropriately.

Written Communication Skills

Occasions for written communication arise frequently and in many forms, from memos to bibliographies. Successful library managers develop their own and their staff members' writing skills.

- Keep in mind the receiver of each message.

- Make an outline of relevant thoughts. Are all relevant points covered? Do the thoughts flow logically? Are there smooth transitional sentences from one thought to another?

- Check spelling and grammar. If desired, use a spelling or grammar checking software program, but do not rely entirely on this method.

- Check the tone of the communication. Project the true meaning of your communication with correct words.

- Express ideas concisely, clearly, and to the point. Avoid redundancy.

- Avoid jargon.

- Use short sentences often. They say more than long sentences.

- Decide on the desired outcome from any written communication. Action or a record for referral? Follow-up or feedback?

- Watch for personal prejudice, distortions, or over-generalizations. Back up opinions with facts.

- Use written communications when details are important in a policy or directive.

- Decide if there is a need for an inexpensive means of providing the same message to a large group. Should each person have a copy of the message or is it sufficient for a designated person to receive a copy and be responsible for communicating the message to the group?

- Decide if a reply to your message is desirable or necessary.

- Summarize major points at the end.

- Learn to express the right degree of intensity for the message. Practice giving emphasis in the proper places to get key points across.

LISTENING Skills

Listen effectively. It plays a large part in everyday activities. Because people spend 90 percent of each day communicating (45 percent of that time is taken up in listening), the quality of work suffers or benefits from how well a person listens. Seldom are people taught to listen effectively or actively. Researchers maintain that a large amount of what people hear is misunderstood, forgotten, or just plain ignored. Using effective listening skills gets people to respond positively.

- Listen passively. Not talking while others are talking to you shows respect by giving them a chance to express themselves.

- Respond with vocal sounds. Vocal sounds such as "uh-huh" and "hmmm," or words such as "really," "right," and "oh" tell others you are listening. This communication of empathy and attention keeps the focus on the message and implies no judgment of the speaker's message.

- Encourage the speaker. Use phrases, words, or sentences that urge the speaker to tell more about the subject. Use such phrases as "Go on," "Tell me more," "Explain how you felt," or "What followed after that?"

Active Listening

Active listening lets people know that others hear what they are saying and feeling. According to Janette Caputo, active listening skills include five techniques.

1. Pay quiet attention to the speaker. Practice "noninterruptive listening." Lean forward, establish eye contact, and nod at appropriate times.

2. Ask open-ended questions that require answers beyond simple "yes" or "no." Open-ended questions help others explore their feelings. For example, a question, "Would you like to organize a program for senior citizens?" allows the respondent to give the affirmative or the negative with little indication of true feelings. If a library manager asked, "How would you feel about helping organize a program for senior citizens?" the answers could range from, "I don't have those skills," to "My mother is quite ill right now, and it would be very depressing to me to work with that age group at this time."

3. "Parrot," or repeat back the same words, occasionally with a change of emphasis. Don't overuse this technique to the point of distraction.

4. Paraphrase. Repeat or summarize what is said, then ask for confirmation of the interpretation. Using the above example, say "Are you saying you would rather plan programs for a different age group at this time?"

5. Reflect the feelings of the speaker, or read between the lines. Explain how it appears the speaker feels, going beyond the actual words spoken. For example, "You must be very worried about your mother." (Caputo 1984, 14)

Successful library managers practice the following techniques to improve their active listening skills.

Ask questions. Include questions that encourage the speaker to give more information as they sense genuine interest. Questions are never indiscreet. Answers sometimes are. Use words such as who, what, when, and where to probe for further meaning.

Restate the communication. When a library manager restates part or all the message, it lets the speaker know he or she has the attention of the listener and fosters mutual understanding of the communication.

Identify goals. Decide on expectations. Set time limits on the listening.

Make preparations. To get the most from a speaker, have a pen, paper, notes, or tape recorder. If using a tape recorder, make sure the speaker grants permission to record the message.

Recognize propaganda and manipulative language. Be alert to how the speaker uses language and opinions.

Know your own prejudices. Have a clear mind. Let no other thoughts intrude. Surrender any preconceived concepts.

Overlook irrelevant factors. If the information presented is not germane to the subject, concentrate on the relevant factors.

Sort out what you listen to. Listen critically to the speaker. Guard against being taken in by fallacies. Ask yourself these questions:

What is the speaker's background?
What message is the speaker trying to get across?
How is the speaker trying to influence the audience?
How is the message related to the subject?
What verbal and nonverbal messages is the speaker
communicating?
Is there anything the speaker is omitting?

Tune out physical distractions such as the speaker's appearance, gestures, or speech habits. Learning to listen requires concentration. Don't allow communication noise such as appearance or demeanor to affect the message.

Guidelines for Improving Listening Skills

The following techniques may help improve listening skills.

Show attentiveness. Make eye contact and do not wander often to other people or objects. Comfortable and attentive eye contact with the speaker conveys interest, and that is important. Do not, however, stare at the speaker because that's an intimidation tactic. A library manager trains to be comfortable with "soft" contact. Avoid glancing around the room because that communicates lack of interest in the speaker's message. Show sensitivity to cultural differences. In some cultures, people interpret direct eye contact as expressing a desire for intimacy; in other cultures, direct eye contact is confrontational.

Use good manners. Avoid actions that may disrupt the speaker's concentration, such as fidgeting, writing, or glancing at the clock. Do not interrupt. Do not ask irrelevant questions or too many questions, which might cause the speaker to lose a train of thought or change the subject. Relax and avoid hints of impatience. Never allow the person to feel intimidated because a cooperative environment could provide more information. If a phone call interrupts a conversation, ask the calling party for permission to return the call. In some facilities, a library manager has the option to direct staff to hold all calls until the end of a conversation.

Concentrate on body language. Some people show positive responses by smiling, raising their eyebrows, nodding their head in agreement, or moving closer to the speaker. One successful body language technique is to lean slightly forward, face the speaker squarely, and take a position at an appropriate, comfortable distance, with arms and legs uncrossed.

Ask important questions. This helps a library manager understand how well he or she is listening. Look for commonality with the speaker. Offer positive reinforcement by complimenting first and giving constructive suggestions later.

Value silence. Silence allows the speaker to set the pace and to choose what and how much information to be share. It also builds trust. Some listeners are uncomfortable with silence and strongly desire to break the silence. When tempted to interrupt, silently review the speaker's previous points and study the speaker's body language.

Be conscious of distractions. Effective library managers select what they hear. Choose to listen to the relevant information and tune out the irrelevant. Attention is an important tool. An attentive library manager will remember more, save time, and cut stress.

Good listening skills enable library managers to more comfortably understand what another person says and means. Don't underrate or neglect this skill. A library manager's job requires constant, effective communication with all people.

Bill is the manager of a special library. A department head requested a special search be done as soon as possible. Bill assigned the task to Susan. At closing, Susan reported that part of the new research was finished, but one request sent by facsimile to another location would not receive a response for a day or two. She asked if the entire search results could allow for two days' delay. Bill nodded. Two days later, the department head telephoned Bill and called him to account for not providing the search results. Bill called Susan into his office and began criticizing her work over the past month, accusing her of distraction.

Puzzled and angry, Susan returned to her desk, pulled out an application she recently completed for another job, and placed a stamp on the envelope. Bill's lack of attention to Susan's previous question and his criticism for no apparent reason resulted in the loss of a good employee.

Additional Steps to Improve Communication

Successful library managers need to know more than the basic facts of effective communication skills. They need to practice.

- Make sure communication with others is authentic. Use words that accurately express feelings and intentions. Keep verbal and nonverbal communications consistent with each other. These actions demonstrate trustworthiness and dependability.

- Have the courage to choose responses to others according to personal values and principles. This acceptance of oneself increases self-esteem and promotes effective communications.

- Recognize that not all people respond in the same way to a situation.

- Focus on a win-win outcome. In a conflict or confrontation situation, use appropriate verbal and nonverbal communication skills. Separate the person from the problem. Emphasize positive intentions. Don't assign blame. Listen actively and avoid misunderstandings by paraphrasing, checking perceptions, and asking for a feeling response. Ask for solutions. For more information, see chapter 6.

- Recognize that 75 percent of all communication is oral (one person speaking and another listening). Listening skills are probably the weakest communication skills, in part because people speak at 100 to 200 words a minute, but they think at 400 to 500 words a minute.

Also practice these communication techniques.

- Use empathy to improve communications. It helps to understand others' feelings and thoughts.

- Strive to genuinely understand what someone communicates.

- Recognize appropriate timing and conditions for effective communications. For example, if there is disruptive news, try to choose a reasonable time and a calm atmosphere.

- Repeat the other person's comments or ideas to obtain unobstructed points of view and maintain the flow of conversation.

- Refrain from verbally attacking others.

- Recognize that perceptions, personalities, attitudes, motives, emotions, self-interest, and abilities influence communications.

Proxemics

Proxemics is "the study of the ways humans use and communicate with space" (Richmond et al. 1991, 118), or the way people arrange themselves in relation to each other in personal, social, and public settings. It includes space and the movement of people within that space.

A skillful library manager takes into consideration staff members' territory and space needs. Richmond and others identified the six categories of territory as primary, secondary, public, home, inter-actional, and body (Richmond et al. 1991, 120). Personal work space considerations allow for distance and insulation and give staff some sense of personal integrity and separation. For example, an office is the primary territory, the private domain of its owner, and one should not enter an employee's office without an invitation.

Secondary territory is no one's private domain, but people asso-ciated its use with a particular group, such as tables in the staff room where certain people regularly sit. Learning to abide by these unspoken rules helps smooth the transition of a new employee into the library.

Cultural norms and personal differences influence people's need for space. Awareness of the distances that people prefer plays a significant role in the effect one person's presence has on others. To establish rapport with another person, don't violate the person's space. Different personality types have different distance require-ments. Extroverts usually feel more comfortable working close to others, and they use more exaggerated gestures. Introverts usually feel more comfortable when given additional space, and their ges-tures are more reserved. In our culture, one and a half to three feet is a comfortable social distance.

The personal space needs of people may reflect living arrange-ments. One can often detect whether people live in a crowded environment or less crowded environment by how close they stand when shaking hands. Being aware of another person's needs may help win the other person's confidence.

To facilitate communication and relationships at meetings, give consideration to the environment. Seek an attractive and comfort-able meeting location. Choose a location in a neutral environment so no territorial problem intimidates the participants. Conversely, to influence others, use the library or media center for meetings.

Seating arrangements within a room are also important. For co-operative working relationships involving two people, set up a side-to-side seating arrangement. For a competitive situation, try an across-the-table arrangement. For casual conversation, use a corner-to-corner seating arrangement. To create an independent working situ-ation for two, use seats at opposite ends of table. To lead a group, be the most active participant. To seek status, occupy the seat at the end of the table. Produce a non-threatening and trusting atmosphere by seating participants around the table with the ends of the table vacant.

Avoid sitting in deep armchairs that compel people to sit in the back of the chair. This eliminates a strong, positive position to interact with others. Sit facing a woman and adjacent to a man to receive a more cooperative response from each.

A successful library manager uses proxemic zones to facilitate better communication and trust among coworkers.

References

Caputo, Janette S. 1984. *The Assertive Librarian.* Phoenix: Oryx Press.

Gensing, Lin. 1991. *Motivating Today's Work Force.* British Columbia: Self-Counsel Press.

Richmond, Virginia P., James C. McCroskey, and Steven K. Payne. 1991. *Nonverbal Behavior in Interpersonal Relations.* 2d ed. Englewood Cliffs, NJ: Prentice-Hall.

8

WORKING WITH ADMINISTRATORS AND OTHER MANAGERS

All library managers report to a higher authority unless they own their own facility. Library managers also work and share experiences with peers in their own or other organizations and agencies. This chapter presents suggestions for working with management colleagues.

Management is often a lonely assignment. Fraternizing with one staff member may make the others suspicious, generating conflict. Networking with others at a peer level, making similar types of decisions, and solving similar problems help relieve stress.

Many different "bosses" exist in the library community. In a public library, directors report to library trustees or a city council, with the president of the trustees being the chief administrator. In larger public libraries, a manager may be responsible for a series of departments. People managing multiple departments may include the manager of branches for a large public library, the manager of technical services, the manager for youth programs, and the manager of reader's services. For a school district, the superintendent is the chief administrator, and principals and other department directors are colleagues of the directors of school library media programs.

This book uses the term "administrator" to describe the person to whom the library director reports, and those at parallel levels are titled "colleagues."

Understanding the Roles of Colleagues

An important part of establishing a good relationship with colleagues is to understand their work environment by learning the answers to the following questions.

What are the professional goals of these colleagues? Will they share a list of short- and long-range goals? Some organizations publish stated goals and use them to evaluate relevant programs and personnel. If not, a library manager must patiently research the objectives and goals of their organizations to identify ways to work together for mutually beneficial outcomes.

Bob, an energetic young adult librarian, meets annually with his director to discuss Bob's goals. Bob always knows his director's professional goals for the year and provides a goal of his own to enhance one of his director's. This promotes a close working relationship between the two professionals.

What are the commitments of your colleagues? Determine the priorities and commitments of colleagues for their organizations, their professions, their immediate community, and their wider community. Also consider their more personal priorities, such as hobbies and sports interests. All this takes patience and time. Use direct conversation, effective listening, committee membership, joint meetings, shared functions, and direct research to learn about your colleagues' priorities.

What kinds of power do your colleagues have? Colleagues often have access to people in "high places." A library manager needs to understand how the power of colleagues influences personal career advancement and provides support for an organization's projects. Determining how willing colleagues are to exercise their power for others helps a library manager make good human resource decisions. Colleagues affect the operation of the library by facilitating personal and organizational recognition.

Colleagues may have access to budget resources, including private and public funds. Join them in projects to expand resources, programs, collections, and special resources of the library. Knowing the kinds of power colleagues hold gives a clearer understanding of what to expect in a working relationship with them.

What are the strengths and weaknesses of your colleagues? Acknowledging the strengths and weaknesses of colleagues allows library managers to work toward enhancing strengths and repairing weaknesses of their own. Positive attitudes and energies enhance everyone's performance. When one colleague is very weak, try to find out the source. It could be only a lack of confidence. Be alert to clues in conversation. If a colleague's life experiences are a major contributing factor to his or her weakness, talking to family or associates may help. Weaknesses based on personal situations are difficult to address, but it doesn't help to ignore them.

Show support by sincerely including someone as part of the team. This makes everyone a winner. Everyone has weaknesses, and how library managers handle things is important. If one person is overly emotional or aggressive, others should try to remain non-reactive. Understanding the motives for behaviors helps people know how to respond. Always give positive and encouraging feedback whenever possible to show both loyalty and respect.

What is your colleague's communication style? Ascertain whether a colleague prefers formal or casual communication. Some people like to communicate on a face-to-face basis, while others prefer written reports or written requests. When colleagues prefer oral interaction, respond in person and follow up with a detailed, written response or report. If the colleague prefers written communication, respond with written memos. It is important to keep colleagues informed, regardless of the preferred communication style. To support staff members and library programs, colleagues need to know what is happening in the manager's specific library and the organization as a whole. All library managers need to communicate often and clearly with colleagues. Anyone asked to support the goals and objectives of public and school libraries must thoroughly understand the expectations of the job. Their approval and willingness to actively participate in the project is imperative for success. Support each other's positions whenever possible.

What are your colleagues' needs and personal style? Learning about needs and personal styles allows a person to be sensitive to them. Every manager expects certain things from colleagues, such as trust, sensitivity to available time and pressures, dependability, responsibility, and loyalty.

What do your colleagues expect from you? Support is a two-way street. When a library manager builds networks, the time comes when someone asks for help. A library manager must determine the available time and effort before joining colleagues outside the agency. In some instances, a library manager must know the limits of financial resources available for another person's project. When a library manager must refuse a project, provide a clear explanation to retain their support in the future.

Understanding the Role of the Administrator

In addition to understanding colleagues' expectations, review relationships with members of governing boards who ultimately evaluate the performance of library managers. This includes administrators and members of public library boards and the superintendent and administrative staff in a school library. A library manager must care about meeting the needs of these people.

Search for ways to satisfy expectations. Complete projects on time, meet information requests in a reasonable length of time, and remain well organized. The good performance of a library manager reflects on the people who made the decision to hire and reflects on the quality of library services being offered. Be trustworthy. Be dependable, responsible, and loyal to those in authority. All library managers need to be able to trust their administrators, and administrators need to be able to trust their managers. When library managers perform their jobs in an exemplary manner, it relieves the administrators of worry about this aspect of their responsibility. A good library manager takes the initiative to perform well. No one needs to ask them for good performance. As a loyal employee and a good team player, library managers support their administrators.

It helps to know the personal interests and recreational needs of an administrator. How they choose to relax tells a great deal about aspects of their personalities and facilitates adjustments of working and personal relationships with a library manager.

It does not take long to find out if an administrator's personal style is goal-oriented or people-oriented. Whatever the style, react to it accordingly. If their style is formal, respond in a formal manner. When the style is more casual or people oriented, rely on less formal meetings.

As a library manager, recognize the administrator's fundamental management and leadership abilities. Organizations expect administrators to excel as managers and leaders. If they do not, library managers can help by showing expertise, problem solving in creative ways, and managing the library well. Answering the following questions may help.

1. Does the administrator help the organization feel like a team?

Chapter 4 discusses ways to build a team. When an administrator does not have team-building skills, a library manager can either encourage this type of behavior from the administrator, or a library manager can build the team and share it with the administrator.

2. Does the administrator seem vaguely embarrassed by a leadership role?

Almost all appointments have a political basis at some point along the way. This means that some administrators may be better politicians than they are leaders. An administrator who is shy about leading needs a strong manager who will lead but also give the illusion that the administrator is actually leading the organization.

3. Is the administrator open to new ideas and adaptable to changes?

An administrator who is rooted in tradition and reluctant to make any changes is a dangerous deterrent to meeting the needs of library patrons in this modern society. A clever library manager places improvements in the context of tradition to make the proposed change appear less radical. Call it an "upgrade" instead of a "new" method. Asking people to "test" a new method is usually more successful than asking them to "change" their system.

4. Does the administrator enjoy and understand his or her role?

New and veteran administrators attend sessions at professional associations to help them become better at their jobs. A good library manager strives to work with an administrator for progress by relating successful outcomes and pointing out problems. For every problem brought to an administrator, offer a possible solution.

5. Can this person handle the position well?

It is difficult for a library manager and the staff members to carry out their duties if the administrator cannot handle his or her position well. When an administrator is unable to adequately fill the role, a library manager must work even harder to see that the library does not suffer.

6. Is this person accessible for meetings?

When an administrator is inaccessible, prepare written communications asking for confirmation of decisions made and changes to be implemented. Keep written copies of such correspondence to document the steps followed in maintaining library services.

7. Does the administrator use conflict constructively or avoid it at all costs?

Administrators who avoid conflict will certainly push that conflict onto a library manager. Watch any constructive conflict situation closely to see that the conflict does, in fact, achieve consensus in a timely fashion.

8. Are the administrator's decision-making skills participative, open, and flexible, or dictatorial and authoritative?

In an open environment, an administrator expects teams to solve problems. A library manager builds a team and uses the team process to achieve consensus during problem solving. When an administrator is a dictator, a library manager must carry out "orders" and employ advanced people skills when the "order" lacks probability of success. Unfortunately, most dictators consider lack of success a problem of those implementing an order rather than the order itself.

9. Does the administrator shift management styles often, leaving others confused as to his or her style?

Administrators who profess to be one type of manager but are, in effect, the exact opposite confuse people only a little less than those who switch management styles on a whim. Shifting management styles leads to staff "testing" the atmosphere before determining how to approach a situation. This produces ineffective management, and the administrator needs to attend some management training sessions. The hard part is planting the suggestion in a way that makes an administrator think it's his or her own idea. Watch for appropriate workshops, send for pamphlets, and suggest ideas.

After determining an administrator's management style, use chapter 4 to create a strategy for working together and a plan to get the staff included in decision making. It is more difficult to integrate a staff into the decision-making process of an autocratic administrator than a democratic one.

10. Would the administrator be a better team leader if a library manager becomes a better team player?

An experienced library manager periodically reviews team-building performance. A good team leader can say they've helped most of the staff work together on small and large projects. A better leader knows when to follow someone else's leadership. Knowing when to lead and when to follow is an essential skill. Modeling this for an administrator may help that person grow as an effective team person.

Joe, a private school administrator, assumed sole responsibility for making budget cuts for instructional supplies one year, and teacher morale suffered greatly.

The next year, Joe gained a lesson in more effective administration with the help of Gigi, a K-12 library media specialist. In a department chairperson meeting on allocation of the instructional supply budget, Gigi suggested that each department prioritize and submit their requests in writing.

At the next meeting, she put the dollar figures for each budget request on a board for everyone's review. The requests exceeded the building's instructional supply budget. Gigi offered to give up a percent of her budget to meet the pressing need for instructional software for the new math curriculum. Other department chairs made similar sacrifices and adjustments, and the group achieved a balanced budget plan.

The following year, Gigi reminded the group of that substantial budget cut she accepted to support a crucial curriculum need and asked for their reciprocal support for new encyclopedias on CD-ROM. Gigi got all she wanted and more.

---

11. How can you help an administrator excel?

Remember that it doesn't make any difference who gets the credit as long as the project is successful. A good library manager provides information concerning successful programs in the library to an administrator without worrying about personal benefit or glory. The best thing that can happen to a library manager is that the program gets publicity as a successful venture. If an administrator gets or takes the credit, that's fine. The library program is still the ultimate winner.

Library programs and staff improve and grow under an effective library manager. When the program is running smoothly, an administrator has the support necessary to ask for additional funding so that the program can grow.

Expanding Effective Communications

Everyone benefits when communication lines are open, effective, clear, and efficient among all levels of personnel within and without an organization. Clarify first if there are any communication problems. Effective library managers assess interpersonal relations with colleagues and their administrators. They look for any communication habits that need modification or elimination.

If communication problems exist, request a meeting. Find appropriate times to meet when few interruptions will occur. Avoid meetings during any other crisis for the administrator because such distractions will disrupt the administrator's concentration, will reduce the chance of a focused discussion, and may adversely impact any decisions.

Send a premeeting memo concerning perceived communication problems. During the meeting, be an active listener and be aware of the nonverbal communications sent and received. Watch for body language. Good posture, forward-leaning body position, pleasant facial expressions, good eye contact, and a relaxed manner suggest positive reactions. Strained facial expressions, frequent glances around the room or at the clock, crossed arms, nervous fingers, or hand motions suggest negative reactions. If the atmosphere becomes negative, ask for another meeting at a more favorable time or ask those at the meeting how they feel about what is being discussed. Ask probing questions to trigger more concentration on the conversation.

During meetings, listen carefully to avoid misunderstandings. Be prepared to paraphrase, summarize, and find points for mutual agreement. Before leaving any meeting, be sure everyone understands clearly any decisions. Take notes on matters discussed or decisions made. Record the time and date on the notes. If possible, use a laptop computer to record such information.

When meeting with non-librarians, avoid library jargon and the use of acronyms. It is poor manners to make things difficult, and people get very annoyed when they don't understand the discussion.

Don't dump responsibility for solving problems or making presentations on individuals or groups without offering one or two possible solutions. Put the ideas in writing, prepare a bulleted list, or draw a diagram. Visual (not just verbal) suggestions help everyone think through the problem and make communication clearer.

Be specific when asking for support. Approach a request for favor slowly. Get agreement on several matters and then ask for support. The old adage "By the inch, it's a cinch; by the yard, it's hard" applies to achieving results. Make sure a proposal or idea has a chance before asking for cooperation. Present it from a positive point of view. It may be necessary to lobby ahead of time and build a base. Expect everyone to ask "what's in it for them." Prepare compromises or rewards to encourage people to sign onto a project.

Review the discussion at each meeting to determine if there is a resolution to the problem. If the group reaches a conclusion, repeat the finding to confirm the assumption. End all meetings in a spirit of cooperation. Thank people for time spent helping to solve the problem.

Verbal or written follow-ups to meetings are essential products of effective library management, providing a record of attendance, discussions, and agreements. Record the date and time of the meeting. If a library manager is not the one who provides the summary, he or she should carefully review the summary for completeness.

Always respect the time of others by being brief with any presentation or request. If it is a new plan, simply explain what it can do and give colleagues time to think it over.

Effective library managers also practice communications outside of meetings. Offer to write articles for newspapers or community bulletins, the school district newsletter, or other media. Maintain accurate records and vital statistics for administrators and board members to show achievement of the organization's goals. Use records and statistics to show that the library program is important to the community. Offer to attend meetings and represent the administration or give speeches to organizations to explain the importance and function of the library. Volunteer to help administrators and board members with speeches by researching statistics and drafting presentations.

HelpiNq StAff UNdERstANd AdMiNistRAtive PoiNT-of-View

Communicating administrative needs to staff members helps them understand the "big picture." With the knowledge of the needs, strengths, weaknesses, and personal styles of other managers and administrators, staff supports a library manager's efforts and helps the administrator become a better team player. For example, if staff members know the board president is a perfectionist, they can predict and plan to support a distinct management style that expects precise and thorough completion of projects and assignments.

Library managers are more successful if those surrounding them are successful. This includes patrons of the library, staff, administrators, board members, and other managers. The entire institution and the library management profession flourish when supporting factors are successful.

9

CONDUCTING SUCCESSFUL WORKSHOPS, PRESENTATIONS, AND MEETINGS

Library managers often conduct workshops, give presentations, run meetings, and plan and conduct successful public appearances. In addition to superior skills in communications, organization, conflict management, problem solving, time management, and team building are prerequisites, successful library managers develop strategies for each specific assignment.

PRESENTATIONS

One of the best methods for marketing library services is to tell an audience what the library has to offer. Various community groups, boards, and other organizations often invite library managers to tell the library story. "Selling" the library in this way requires an effective, interesting presentation.

Library managers who facilitate successful activities and programs within their libraries should share these with other librarians. Managers with specialized skills or newly implemented technology often share their innovations and expertise with others, and this usually translates into presentations and workshops.

Planning an Effective Presentation

Many people worry about speaking before an audience. Follow these suggestions on planning an effective presentation to gain confidence and reduce fears:

Determine the objectives. Assess the audience or participants in terms of age, experience, common interests, professional objectives, and opinions. Tailor the presentation to the needs, interests, and goals of the audience. Have a clear message for the audience. Decide if persuasion is the primary goal. Know the allotted time for delivery of the information. Predetermine factors to evaluate levels of success.

Prepare the materials and the room. If possible, arrange the room to suit your audience and the type of presentation (lecture, fund raising, open house, etc.). Reserve or obtain all necessary equipment (overhead projector, videocassette recorder, slide projector, microphone, lectern, computer system, flip chart, etc.). Determine the types and quantities of training materials you need (handouts, overhead transparencies, slides, videocassette tapes, music, evaluation forms or tests, etc.).

If using visual aids, ensure they are professional-looking and large enough for the entire audience to read. Check carefully for spelling and grammatical errors. Desktop publishing programs are ideal for creating effective, exciting visual aids. Visual aids should present one relevant idea at a time. Place no more than eight horizontal lines on each transparency, and use slides sparingly because a darkened room isolates a speaker from the audience.

Prepare the presentation. Begin by arranging topics in the order of presentation, keeping the objectives in mind. In the introduction, a library manager should provide a brief explanation of his or her job and cite relevant experience. Memorize the opening and closing statements. In simple terms, tell your audience what you are going to tell them. Then tell them. Finally, summarize by telling the audience what you told them. Don't read your speech. Use notes only for the main part of the presentation, and make sure they are small (5" x 7" cards are good) and easily handled at a lectern. If the facilities do not include a lectern or equivalent, reduce any dependency on notes.

Presentation titles are important. Keep it short, and make it relevant to goals and objectives. Avoid clichés and cute expressions, but word it to draw attendance. Some good titles show action or suggest solutions. Make the title easy to remember.

During preparation and presentation, consider the following tips.

- Be positive (this commands respect).

- Be punctual.

- Keep within the allotted time.

- Be well rehearsed.

- Dress appropriately.

- Be aware that local news people may be attending the meeting.

- Stand when making the presentation.

- Be sure the information is accurate.

- Use professionally made visual aids when possible.

- Tie in references to the community if possible.

- Know the agenda, especially other topics that may be discussed.

- Do not use jargon or read the presentation. Do not put members on the spot or ask for special privileges during the meeting.

- Keep the presentation closure clearly in mind.

Tape your speech and listen to the sentence phrasing. Practice with a microphone, and learn how to hold it so that it does not echo or squeal. Investigate several types microphones and identify the pros and cons of each. Some speakers prefer a microphone that they can raise or lower to the appropriate height on a podium or a stage. Others prefer a lapel microphone to leave their hands free and allow greater mobility. A hand-held microphone permits range of movement but is a burden for long presentations.

Delivering an Effective Presentation

Joe, a public librarian, presented the annual budget request to the governing board. Through careful planning, Joe began with requests for normal library expenditures, presenting evaluative data from each major event. Next, Joe proposed a new project, one that might be controversial. He displayed charts that demonstrated the success of other new projects authorized by this board.

Reassured of the soundness of their previous judgments on new projects , the board approved the new budget.

On the day of any presentation, arrive early and check out equipment, accessibility of outlets, lighting, room arrangements, water, and exits. If the presentation includes slides, ensure their correct sequence and smooth feed in the projector. A little tool kit, even a small Swiss army knife, can come in handy. Is there enough light to read notes or outlines when the lights are dimmed? Wear comfortable clothing. Some speakers prefer to distribute evaluation sheets and handouts prior to the presentation to avoid awkward and time-consuming interruptions during the talk. Other speakers prefer not to give handouts to the audience to keep audience attention on the speaker, not the papers.

Don't worry overmuch about the content of the presentation. It naturally follows all the preparations. A library manager knows a need exists for the idea or program because he or she was invited or approved to present the information. The advance work of planning what will be said, preparing visual aids and handouts, and practicing to fit within the allotted time establishes a strong foundation for the actual presentation. It's no secret that logical preparation bestows confidence.

Beginning the presentation. An appropriate opening graciously and sincerely acknowledges the presence of the chairperson and honored guests. Don't mention stage fright or nervousness. Stand quietly and assume a posture of calm confidence. Most audiences are empathetic. Expect to give an effective presentation or speech. Don't be pessimistic. Visualize success.

The middle of a presentation. Apply communications skills throughout the presentation. Deliver the material in a natural, conversational tone, varying the tempo of the speech. Insert pauses from time to time to give credence to the subject and validity to the shared knowledge. Energy and enthusiasm puts an audience on the speaker's side every time. If something goes wrong, relax and make a joke of it. Restate or summarize the information and continue. Be positive and friendly. Remember to use "I" sparingly and "you" frequently.

Make eye contact with someone in the audience, preferably someone whose attention inspires confidence. Change eye contact from time to time to another member of the audience.

Don't stand in one place unless required by an immovable microphone. Balance your stance and attention between the audience on the left and the audience on the right. Don't favor one side of the room over another. Move close to the audience at intervals, especially to focus on one participant to answer a question. Planned movement during a presentation requires advance arrangements for a lapel or hand-held microphone.

Watch the time. Stay in control if there is audience participation. If the presentation is longer than 30 minutes, plan a break of some type. A successful presentation blends time for delivery with time for integration and evaluation.

Ending the presentation. Give an audience some clue that the end is nearing with a summary. Deliver a very strong and positive finish, one that is meticulously prepared and memorized. Allow for a question-and-answer period, if possible.

Try to finish earlier than the audience anticipated, and let them know they have a few minutes to interact with other participants or the speakers. Control the length of the question period. If there are not enough handouts, pass out envelopes and ask participants to self-address them and indicate the handouts they want, or provide a sign-up sheet for names, addresses, and requests for additional materials. Always thank the audience and those responsible for the invitation.

Workshops and In-Service Training

Conducting workshops and in-service training is a major responsibility for many library managers. In smaller organizations, library managers and staff often plan and present workshops for the benefit of others working in the library, including part-time employees and volunteers. Library managers also present workshops for audiences outside the library.

A successful workshop imparts new knowledge to an audience in a stimulating and motivating way. Planning and implementing workshops usually requires strong efforts from two primary contributors: the person who sponsors and organizes the workshop and the person who presents it. The steps for planning workshops and the factors to consider for implementation are similar to those previously presented for presentations.

Planning an Effective Workshop

Organizing a workshop requires financial planning. Prepare a budget, taking into consideration the length of the workshop, materials necessary for the workshop and for each participant, facilities, refreshments, accommodations, and speaking fees. Determine whether to charge a fee for workshop participation. Offer specific compensation to workshop presenters or let them know that none is available.

After resolving financial matters, planners must prepare the facility. Is there adequate and comfortable seating? Can participants practice hands-on techniques covered in the workshop? Are there desks or tables for notetaking?

Consider the timing of the workshop. Ideally, a library manager should select a time that doesn't conflict with another exceptional workshop, activity, or speaker. Try to schedule workshops early in the day or early in the conference, when participants will be fresh and attentive. Schedule periodic breaks or periods of physical activity to keep everyone alert. Make sure any supplied beverages and food accommodate a variety of preferences.

Don't forget to prepare some means for evaluating the effectiveness of a workshop. Elicit constructive comments from the audience and make improvements for the next presentation.

After organizing the workshop, begin planning the content of the program. Remember that an effective workshop

- taps participants' previous experiences and provides new experiences. Learning is a blend of old ideas with new ones.

- is problem-centered. It poses issues that are important to participants and gives them direct experience in dealing with the issues.

- is entertaining. The presenter should include some humor, such as an appropriate scenario to prove a point.

- is filled with successful experiences that build confidence and reinforce positive attitudes.

- blends time for delivery of information with time for integration and evaluation of learning. Workshops require two-way interactions.

- offers a variety of activities that allow participants to use different learning styles.

- helps participants clarify options and then helps them select from the options. If participants leave a workshop with more questions than answers, they may not use what they have learned.

- helps participants develop new competencies. People should leave a workshop believing they can do something they could not do before they came.

MEETINGS

Good meetings are time saved, not wasted. Call meetings only when necessary and prepare a written agenda. Send a notice of the meeting to the attendees and clearly state the purpose of the meeting and the agenda. Include procedures and time expectations for the meeting. To promote participation, ask for additional agenda items and allow time for discussion of concerns at the meeting. Keep the meeting focused on the agenda. If discussion wanders off the agreed-upon topics, a library manager must redirect attention to issues on the agenda.

If a library manager starts the meeting on time, people learn to arrive on time. Do not repeat information for those who come late. A reporter may take notes and distribute them later to participants.

If unable to attend, a library manager should appoint a responsible person to lead the meeting. After the meeting begins, do not monopolize the meeting: try to involve everyone. If appropriate, try to give everyone a chance to contribute. Do not talk down to anyone. Respect all suggestions, recommendations, or discussions and recognize that meetings can boost morale. If there is bad news, sandwich it in the middle: Never begin or end a meeting on a negative note.

End meetings on time with this question: "Did we achieve the intended objective of the meeting?" If all problems were not solved, set another meeting,, initiate an agenda with the unresolved issues, and solicit additional ideas.

Providing a Healthy Meeting Climate

A healthy meeting climate includes the following conditions:

- Objectives are shared, and participants work as a team.

- Hidden agendas, games, and conflicts are recognized and confronted if they are disrupting the meeting.

- Participants show respect for each other and their ideas.

- Participants attack problems and not each other.

- A high degree of trust is present among participants.

- Participants are goal oriented and do not get easily distracted from accomplishing the goals of the meeting.

- Communications are open and genuine.

- Participants band together during a crisis or in making difficult decisions.

- Participants are cohesive but allow for individuality.

- Those affected by the decisions made in a meeting are included in the meeting or in some phase of the decision-making process whenever possible.

- Participants recognize that the process for making decisions can be almost as important as the actual decision.

- Participants consider several alternatives before making final decisions.

- Participants evaluate the short- and long-range consequences of decisions before finalizing decisions.

- Participants make consensus decisions whenever possible.

- Participants make decisions and assign responsibility for carrying out the decisions before adjourning.

Recognizing the Types of Decisions Made in Meetings

Library managers make decisions by compromise, by consensus, or by force. In decisions by compromise, individual participants engage in give and take to reach a decision that everyone will accept.

For decisions by consensus, participants discuss issues openly, explore disagreements, and consider alternatives until the group reaches a consensus. Consensus decision are usually the most effective kind because they have the most support.

Decisions reached by force may come from a powerful individual or group. An influential team member, possibly the supervisor, may use power or position to win, or a majority or minority of the group may band together and control the decisions.

Making Effective Decisions in Meetings

At the beginning of the meeting, discuss its purpose and identify the problems to be solved. Summarize ideas, check perceptions and feelings, and evaluate interpersonal processes during the meeting.

By the end of the meeting, participants should have a clear understanding of any decisions and the identity of the people responsible for carrying out the decisions. When possible, keep a written record of the meeting details.

Effectively planned and implemented workshops, presentations, and meetings can do much to further the careers of library managers, particularly in a healthy meeting climate. Spend time considering the goals of the audience, the sponsors, and the speakers and use effective management tools to make the workshops, presentations, and meetings as beneficial as possible for the staff and the library as a whole.

10

EFFECTIVE
LEADERSHIP SKILLS

LibRARY MANAgERS AS LEAdERS

Library managers, if they are to be truly effective, need to be leaders and managers. This chapter describes a library manager as leader and defines the differences between managers and leaders. In *Secrets of Effective Leadership,* Fred Manske shows us

Leaders Tend to . . .
Stress relationships with others, values and commitment—the emotional and spiritual aspects of the organization.
Managers Tend to . . .
Stress organization, coordination and control of resources (e.g., plant, equipment, and people).

Leaders Tend to . . .
Create and articulate a vision of what the organization could achieve in the long run.
Managers Tend to . . .
Focus on achieving short-term objectives and goals.

Leaders Tend to . . .
Move the organization in new directions by being
unsatisfied with maintaining the status quo
Managers Tend to . . .
Concentrate on maximizing results from existing
functions and systems.

Leaders Tend to . . .
Communicate the purpose of doing things
Managers Tend to . . .
Communicate directives, policies and procedures.

Leaders Tend to . . .
Favor taking risks and making changes.
Managers Tend to . . .
Fear uncertainty and act cautiously.

Leaders Tend to . . .
Generate a feeling of meaning in work, including its
value and importance. .
Managers Tend to . . .
Enforce fulfillment of agreements and contracts for
work.

(1987, 6)

The Functions of a Leader

In *Leadership Skills* (1990, 376), William Tracey lists the three basic functions of leaders as

- creating and communicating a vision

- taking action to improve performance

- taking action to improve organizational and human relationships

If library leaders are to create visions, improve performance, and build relationships, their job descriptions must include these functions. The descriptions and definitions of leaders are often similar regardless of who writes them. In her description of a leader, Marlene Caroselli describes a leader as one who develops teams, energizes, shares knowledge, motivates, investigates, enlivens, organizes, is mature, is self-confident, is ethical, envisions, follows through, communicates, actualizes, is intelligent, and welcomes change (1990, 5-22). Warren Bennis and Burt Nanus describe a leader as a broker of the needs of constituencies both within and outside the organization and as someone who is responsible for a set of ethics (1985, 186). They also believe that leaders have the capacity "to develop and improve their skills" (59).

Leadership qualities that yield long-term results by combining these and other theorists' views include communication skills; shared knowledge, vision, accountability; self-esteem and self-respect; integrity; ethical judgment; perseverance; accessibility; and respect. A library leader also enables others, investigates, motivates, follows through, disciplines, enlivens and energizes with zest and flexibility, and achieves results.

Possesses communication skills and shares knowledge. Effective library leadership requires excellent communication skills. Staffs who understand and share vision, mission, and goals will work harder to accomplish them. Exercising good communication skills also helps a library leader share knowledge with members of the group.

Has a vision. Good library leaders possess a vision that provides purpose and direction. Their vision is based on and supported by well-defined values. Library leaders must articulate their vision to their staff and library patrons. One leadership tip is for library managers to write a comprehensive description of their vision and a list of associated values, reflecting how daily actions echo and reinforce those values. Constant review of progress toward the vision allows library managers to analyze their management style and its effect on those they work with.

A library manager's vision should support the organization's goals, and the mission statement should flow from the vision. The vision must be shared with others, especially if they were not part of the development of the vision, the mission statement, or the statement of goals. Reflect the vision in job descriptions and daily assignments and incorporate it into library activities.

Because the library system was very large, the director asked the branch library managers to attend a planning meeting each year and bring one or two staff members with them. The director asked the attendees to review the strategic long-range plan for the library. At the meeting, they discussed the plan and how it could help them meet goals. They considered new objectives to add to the plan, and library managers reviewed their progress toward meeting their goals. The agenda included explanation and discussion of changes in services and additions or cuts in budgets. New trends in information services were reviewed.

Each manager and representative subsequently held a meeting at their own library to discuss this annual review with the remainder of the staff. This process facilitated dissemination of important organizational information to each staff member and reinforced an understanding of the vision for library services in the city.

If staff members are encouraged to adopt the vision so that it also becomes their vision, they will accept responsibility for helping to achieve it. The vision, mission, and goals should be documented and displayed as visual reminders. Successful leaders create a feeling of unity in direction.

Visions accommodate the culture of the organization, and any abrupt changes in the vision, mission, or goals that are contrary to the culture of the organization will cause discomfort in the staff. For example, it may be difficult to instantly establish a democratic environment after replacing an autocratic leader who dictated each person's tasks for many years.

Follows through. Successful leaders must implement their visions. They must follow through by designing activities and monitoring implementation and results.

Is accountable. Library leaders understand that they are accountable to both their staff and their management. Leaders work to achieve the goals of the organization while supporting the goals of the staff under their direction.

Enables others to act. James Kouzes and Barry Posner (1991, 131) added this quality to the generally accepted definitions of leadership. They say that leaders know that they cannot do it alone. Because it takes partners to get extraordinary things done in organizations, leaders build teams with spirit and cohesion, teams that feel like family. They actively involve others in planning and give them discretion to make independent decisions. Leaders make others feel like owners, not hired hands.

Library leaders also develop collaborative goals and cooperative relationships with colleagues. They are considerate of the needs and interests of others. They know that relationships are keys that unlock support for projects. They make sure that when they win, everyone wins. Mutual respect sustains extraordinary group efforts.

Leaders create an atmosphere of trust and human dignity in library facilities. They promote self-esteem for their staff and present them as strong and capable people. Giving staff a sense of being strong and capable is a valuable enabling skill.

Perseveres. Effective library leaders complete tasks required for achieving successful visions, missions, and goals. They work steadily, even when obstacles intervene. Teaming urgency with enthusiasm helps accomplish difficult goals.

Investigates. To motivate staff, innovative investigation skills are required. A library leader must understand the staff from many levels, including personal and professional. The effective leader asks discrete questions, maintains an open-door policy, and carefully listens to employees to determine whether problems facing the staff members at home affect performance at work. However, managers must maintain a high level of professional integrity and ensure full compliance with human resource guidelines for communications with employees. The legal consequences of cultural insensitivity, sexual harassment, and job discrimination are significant. Managers should attend special workshops and refresher courses that provide essential, updated information on these matters.

An effective library leader also investigates and assesses the level of acceptance by staff for goals and proposed activities that support the mission of the library.

Motivates. "Leaders believe in what they are doing. . . . The motivator helps his followers understand the passion he feels for a given undertaking. In time, ideally, that passion will lead to precision on the part of others. As they become more and more involved in a pursuit, they become self-directed" (Caroselli 1990, 8). A library leader must be passionate about the library and its goals and transmit that passion to staff; otherwise, there is risk of rebellion instead of self-direction from the staff.

Demonstrates personal discipline. To meet established goals, leaders must focus on planning and completing specific tasks. A disciplined leader has the ability to concentrate on a task and ensure its completion through personal accomplishment or delegation.

Enlivens and energizes with zest and flexibility. An effective library leader has a strong sense of purpose, with energy for the task. The leader attacks problems, turns them into opportunities, and displays a zest for learning. A flair for the dramatic can energize an organization. Good library leaders are flexible and open to change if different methods are needed to achieve an objective.

Produces results. Good library leaders must translate good intentions into reality and produce results. One effective technique is to employ the highest quality people available to tackle a task. Non-leaders surround themselves with people less skillful or talented than themselves, hoping to "look better" in a situation. A good leader knows it does not matter who gets the credit as long as the task is accomplished, and success is more likely if competent people work on the project.

Possesses self-esteem and self-respect. Leaders, according to Bennis and Nanus (1985, 187), exude self-regard. People who lack self-esteem and self-respect cannot increase the self-esteem of their staff. People with self-respect give and take constructive criticism and consider it an opportunity for growth, thereby improving their performance.

Retains integrity. Integrity is a leadership skill of unparalleled importance. Duplicity will undermine all other efforts at effective leadership. People learn at an early age to recognize when a person is saying one thing and doing another. Good library leaders are honest and sincere in their actions. Manske makes further suggestions related to integrity (1987, 34-36).

- Do what you say you will do.

- Never divulge information given in confidence to you by superiors or colleagues.

- Accept responsibility for your mistakes.

- Never become involved in a falsehood or a lie.

- Avoid accepting gifts or gratuities from inside or outside the company that compromise your ability to perform in the best interest of your employer.

Possesses ethical judgment. Library leaders must see the moral values of a situation and apply therapeutic judgment. "Leaders have a sense of social responsibility. They are concerned with improving the quality of life for many people—not just themselves. . . . Leaders keep an open mind; they try to avoid rigid stereotypical thinking" (Caroselli 1990, 14).

Is accessible. Accessibility is demonstrated by some library managers through an open-door policy. It includes the ability to sincerely listen to others when they are speaking. Accessibility requires a leader to do more than invite people into an office; it needs a leader to listen effectively and communicate successfully an understanding of the message.

Is respected. Library leaders cannot command respect. They must acquire it by demonstration of personal commitment and leadership by example. An effective leader inspires others by believing, setting, demonstrating, and meeting high standards. They perform at the highest level possible, maintain a positive attitude, admit their mistakes, exercise diplomacy, demonstrate commitment as a team player, and seek constantly to improve personal performance.

Leads a Staff. Effective library leaders understand how to motivate others. After establishing the vision, mission statement, and list of goals, a leader motivates staff members and inspires them to achieve excellence. The library leader acts as coach to improve performance, guiding others to present their thoughts and ideas. Employee confidence is built through management demonstrations of trust. Performance incentives facilitate achievement of high standards.

An effective leader produces a staff that can function without a library manager. The staff is willing and eager to collectively function on its own. Successful library leaders look for new and more effective ways to carry out jobs, share ideas for improvement with employees, and provide the necessary training for new technologies and new methodologies.

Staff is motivated by recognition of achievement. An effective library leader looks for success, no matter how small, and rewards it. Leaders thank those who extend extra effort in whatever they do. Showing appreciation engenders loyalty in staff members.

LEADERSHIP STYLES

Leadership styles often fall into the following three categories:

Directive	Participative	Laissez-Faire
Leader makes most decisions	Subordinates are involved in decision	Subordinates make decisions
Responsibility lies with leader	Staff has partial responsibility	Staff has complete responsibility
Communication is vertical	Communication is lateral	Communication is undirected
Leader disciplines	Leader motivates	Self-motivated
Unconcern for feelings	Subordinates' feelings considered	Subordinates' feelings predominant
Task-oriented	People- and group-oriented	Individual-oriented
Leader provides direction	Leader involves the group	Leader provides support
Obedience emphasized	Cooperation emphasized	Independence emphasized

Library managers become better leaders when they understand what leadership style works best for them. Although an individual usually favors one of these leadership styles, specific situations will govern exact usage. There is not always time for a participative decision, and staff members must have complete responsibility for some actions because not everything requires a group decision. Here are a few hints for adopting a leadership style

Mission of the organization. Does the mission statement seem to direct a certain type of leadership style to accomplish the established goals?

The perception of the role. Does the leader feel the responsibility to direct people or to let them take responsibility for their work? Persons who accept management positions should have insight into what is expected in this situation. Too often people fail to see the magnitude of a management position, and, in minimizing its facets, have more difficulty creating a vision.

Beliefs about the people being managed. Is the staff educated and intelligent enough to make most of the decisions wisely? Are the employees well qualified for their jobs? If so, to what degree are they qualified? Clerical staff may need more directive leadership than an employee with a paraprofessional or professional background in libraries.

Leader's level of experience and education in leadership. Is the leader really the person best qualified to lead the discussion on this matter? Is there someone else in the group who has more expertise to whom the leader could defer or with whom the leader could work on this matter?

Value and importance of the job. Is this a critical job with a very high priority? Leaders are seldom micromanagers, those who take responsibility for even the most minute tasks. Because leaders are charged with the task of managing an operation, they must delegate less essential activities. Therefore, leaders direct jobs that are important to the whole picture and spend less energy on smaller jobs.

It is important for a library manager to identify their individual leadership style. Staff recognize leadership traits in those who manage them. Leaders who proclaim themselves one type of leader but who do not exhibit those characteristics will confuse their staff members. The perception survey below may help a library manager recognize their leadership style.

PERCEPTION SURVEY

To improve effectiveness as library managers, it is necessary to learn more about leadership strengths and weaknesses. The "Perception Survey" on pages 121-22 can help a library manager get a more comprehensive picture of how others view their behavior and leadership skills. To obtain the maximum benefits from this survey, give it to staff, coworkers, and administrators and other supervisors in your work environment. Reflect on the answers to each question carefully. Strengths can be measured by the number of times a certain behavior is described as "very good." These are the qualities a library manager wants to build on.

Look at the questions that were answered "poor " or "fair." These reveal areas of behavior that need to be improved. Writing on a separate piece of paper, consider how to transform these behaviors into positive statements; jot down ideas for correcting undesirable behaviors. The goals for behavior changes may be ranked according to their importance to the success of a library manager. Take one step at a time, developing and concentrating first on those that seem the most important or most urgent. Then carefully monitor progress and obtain feedback.

Do not put time limits on specific goals. It takes time to make changes. The important thing is that progress is being made. To assist in the correction of behavior traits, read books on the subject or take courses that will enhance the ability to change specific behaviors.

Conclusion

A library or library media center is often judged by the enthusiasm and energy of a library manager's leadership style and the effectiveness and sensitivity of their professional expertise. This handbook presents people skills that are essential for effective leadership and successful library management, and these skills are effective for library managers with diverse ideas, philosophies, and personalities. I hope library managers will apply these people skills and experience the benefits of improved library management. Good luck and best wishes.

References

Bennis, Warren and Burt Nanus. 1985. *Leaders: The Strategies for Taking Charge*. New York: Harper & Row.

Caroselli, Marlene. 1990. *The Language of Leadership*. Amherst, MA: Human Resource Development Press.

Kouzes, James M., and Barry Z. Posner. 1991. *The Leadership Challenge: How to Get Extraordinary Things Done in Organizations*. San Francisco: Jossey-Bass.

Manske, Fred A. 1987. *Secrets of Effective Leadership*. Memphis, TN: Leadership Education and Development.

Tracey, William R. 1990. *Leadership Skills*. New York: AMACOM.

Appendix:
Perception Survey Handout

Perception Survey

I am conducting a survey to assess how others perceive my behavior so that I may compare your responses with my own perceptions. To this end, I would like your assistance. If you are willing to complete the questionnaire, please accept my thanks and appreciation. The attached candy bar is not a bribe—it's an expression of my appreciation for your time and effort.

It is important that you answer each question thoughtfully and frankly. To ensure complete confidentiality, please do not write your name on the questionnaire. Place the completed questionnaire in the box near the circulation desk by _____ (*date*).

Please evaluate me, _____ (*manager's name*), on a scale of 1 to 5, based on the questions on the next page.

	Very Poor	Poor	Fair	Good	Very Good
My manager	1	2	3	4	5
1. Is friendly and easy to talk with.					
2. Listens well to others whether agreeing or disagreeing.					
3. States points of view of others well.					
4. Encourages others to express their ideas fully.					
5. Encourages others to express their ideas frankly.					
6. Displays confidence and trust in others.					
7. Shares information frankly.					
8. Expects others to do their best.					
9. Sets an example of high standards for personal performance.					
10. Thinks what I do is important.					
11. Encourages innovative and creative ideas.					
12. Is willing to take risks.					
13. Is not defensive when criticized.					
14. Avoids treating others in a condescending manner.					
15. Avoids stating personal views dogmatically.					
16. Avoids dominating discussion.					
17. Avoids being impatient with the progress being made.					
18. Avoids behaving or speaking in a pompous, authoritative manner.					
19. Encourages me to work through disagreements, not suppress them.					
20. Encourages others to work through disagreements, not suppress them.					
21. Uses "we" and "our" rather than "I" or "me" when working in a group situation.					
22. Shows no favorites; treats all equally.					
23. Gives credit and recognition generously.					
24. Accepts more blame than may be warranted for any failure or mistake.					
25. Avoids imposing a decision on a group.					

Index

123